D1176081

A GUIDED TOUR OF RENÉ DESCARTES'
Meditations on First Philosophy

Also by Christopher Biffle:

Landscape of Wisdom: A Guided Tour of Western Philosophy

The Castle of the Pearl: A Guide to Self-Knowledge

Turning Your Life Around (with David Toma)

A Journey Through Your Childhood

Garden in the Snowy Mountains

A Guided Tour of Five Works by Plato, Third Edition

A Guided Tour of Selections from Aristotle's Nicomachean Ethics

Software:

Time Throttle: A Multicultural Tour of the World, 600 B.C.–*1400* A.D.

Also in the Guided Tour Series:

A Guided Tour of John Stuart Mill's Utilitarianism (Julius Jackson, author)

A GUIDED TOUR
OF RENÉ DESCARTES'

Meditations on First Philosophy

THIRD EDITION

with a complete translation of the *Meditations*
by Ronald Rubin

Christopher Biffle

Crafton Hills College

Mayfield Publishing Company
Mountain View, California
London • Toronto

Copyright © 2001, 1996, 1989 by Mayfield Publishing Company

All rights reserved. No portion of this book may be reproduced in any form
or by any means without written permission of the publisher.

Library of Congress Cataloging-in-Publication Data
Biffle, Christopher.
   A guided tour of René Descartes' Meditations on first philosophy / Christopher
Biffle; with a complete translation of the Meditations by Ronald Rubin.—3rd ed.
      p.   cm.
   Includes bibliographical references.
   ISBN 0-7674-0975-2
   1. Descartes, René, 1596–1650. Meditatations de prima philosophia.
2. first philosophy. 3. God—Proof, Ontological. I. Title.
B1854.B54   2000
194—dc21   00-37225
                                                                                        CIP

Manufactured in the United States of America

10   9   8   7   6   5   4   3   2   1

Mayfield Publishing Company
1280 Villa Street
Mountain View, California 94041

Sponsoring editor, Ken King; production editor, Deneen M. Sedlack; manuscript
editor, Jan McDearmon; design manager and cover designer, Glenda King; text
designer, Linda M. Robertson; cover image, The Bettmann Archive; manufacturing
manager, Danielle Javier. The text was set in 10/12 Palatino by Shepherd, Inc.
and printed on acid-free 50# Butte des Morts by The Banta Book Group.

Contents

PREFACE

This book will help your students get the most out of reading Descartes' *Meditations on First Philosophy*. Designed for the novice in philosophy, the text contains Ronald Rubin's complete translation of the *Meditations*, supplemented by tasks that help students develop their philosophical thinking, reading, and writing skills.

My philosophy students need a lot of practice in orderly thinking and writing. They need practice in following a logical pattern, giving reasons for assertions, clarifying points with examples, and quoting supporting material from a text. There is plenty of practice here.

In general, the annotation tasks in the margins are appropriate for a first reading: Students underline key sentences, paraphrase main ideas, and occasionally construct relevant examples. The fill-in-the-blanks dialogues between myself and the reader after each Meditation guide students through rereading and rethinking central passages. These sections may be used as homework assignments (photocopy and hand in), as in-class writing assignments, or as the focus of small-group work.

To help make your student's first encounter with the *Meditations* even more fruitful, I have included the following:

- ❖ A brief introduction to Descartes' life and thought
- ❖ Summaries of each of the six *Meditations*
- ❖ Sections on "Thinking Like Descartes," "Reading Descartes," and "Writing About Descartes"
- ❖ Appendix A, which provides brief selections from Anselm, Aquinas, and Augustine

A WORD ABOUT THE SECOND EDITION

New to the second edition were an extensively revised introduction, a new appendix on argument analysis, many new explanatory notes, annotation tasks, and, most significant, about a hundred new critical-thinking problems in the form of exercises. In general, the exercises begin with tasks designed to give students an overview of each Meditation and then go on to questions involving more detailed analysis. I want to thank the reviewers who gave excellent advice on that edition: Ron Bombardi, Middle Tennessee State University; Geoffrey Frasz, Community College of Southern Nevada; Joram G. Haber, Bergen Community College; Peter King, The

Ohio State University; Michael P. Koch, SUNY Oneonta; Richard Momeyer, Miami University; Robert Sessions, Kirkwood Community College.

NEW TO THE THIRD EDITION

The major improvement in the third edition is the addition of "Your Philosophical Self-Portrait" at the beginning of the *Meditations* and "An Analysis of Your Philosophical Self-Portrait" at the end of the *Meditations*. These exercises function together to help students sketch their own philosophical position and compare it to Descartes'. The major improvement in may own life since the second edition is my wondrous granddaughter, Sophia.

I want to thank my reviewers: Susan Robbins, Rowan University or Eastern College, St. David's, Pennsylvania; Joseph L. Lynch, Cal Poly San Luis Obispo; Dr. Dan Vaillancourt, Loyola University of Chicago; and Dr. Michael A. McMahan, College of the Canyons.

I enjoy hearing from my readers. My e-mail address is CBiffle@aol.com, or you may write me:

Crafton Hills College
Christopher Biffle
11711 Sand Canyon Drive
Yucaipa, CA 92399

ACKNOWLEDGMENTS

This little book would not have been completed without the aid of my colleague Jack Jackson and my best friend, Charles Gary Love. The best ideas in the introduction belong to the former, and the Descartes timeline, the bibliography, and much of the research were contributed by the latter. A few more words, however, need to be added about Gary. No one ever had a better friend. In thirty-one years, there has been no argument between us; those who know us both will guarantee the credit is his.

Christopher Biffle
Yucaipa, California

To C. G. Love.

Francis Bacon on the era of Descartes—

"Nay, the same Solomon the king, although he excelled in the glory of treasure and magnificent buildings, of shipping and navigation, of service and attendance of fame and renown, and the like, yet he maketh no claim to any of those glories, but only to the glory of inquisition of truth; for so he saith expressly, 'The glory of God is to conceal a thing, but the glory of the king is to find it out'; as if, according to the innocent play of children, the Divine Majesty took delight to hide his works to the end to have them found out; and as if kings could not obtain a greater honor than to be God's play-fellows in that game."

The Advancement of Learning, 1605

INTRODUCTION

DESCARTES AND THE RENAISSANCE

One of the easiest ways to understand the Renaissance (1330–1650) is to see that Columbus' voyage to North America in 1492 was a typically Renaissance activity. From the fourteenth to the seventeenth century, exploration of new worlds characterized human activities not only in sea voyages but also in art, architecture, literature, religion, science, and philosophy. Like Columbus, Renaissance explorers left the old world behind, used incomplete maps to find new places, and radically extended the horizons of human knowledge. Descartes' *Meditations,* in the spirit of his age, can be seen as an attempt to plant old values upon new ground.

Near the beginning of the fourteenth century, Giotto, a painter from Florence, Italy, began to explore a new kind of painted world. His figures, unlike those of his predecessors and contemporaries, were three-dimensional, subtly shaded, lifelike. Giotto's Virgin seemed to be sitting on her throne, rather than, in the medieval fashion, awkwardly attached to it. His baby Jesus looked like an infant rather than a miniature adult. Giotto's painfully dead Christ looked as if he had once been vigorously alive; Christ in the Middle Ages looked as ghostly living as dead. Thus, Giotto discovered a new dramatic space. Whereas the medieval artist wanted the viewer to recall the pain of Christ's death, Giotto created a painted space in which the death was reenacted. Under his hand, religious art changed from a collection of holy signs to a window on a religious drama. Giotto's drama on the other side of the window was the new world that other Renaissance artists explored.

At the beginning of the fifteenth century, Filippo Brunelleschi, then an unsuccessful Italian architect, traveled to Rome and began to take measurements of thousand-year-old Roman buildings. Apparently, no one had ever done such a thing. Nearly twenty years later, Brunelleschi created the first piece of Renaissance architecture. On top of the medieval Cathedral of Florence, he erected a dome inspired by his Roman studies. In other words, he erected a pagan space on top of a Christian building. To some eyes, the result looked as odd as it sounds. But Brunelleschi became one of the first Renaissance explorers to establish a solution for other adventurers of the new age: Use an old map, gotten from the Romans (who got theirs from the Greeks), to found a new place.

The development of the theater from the Middle Ages to the seventeenth century is a good example of the Renaissance exploration of new worlds. With the collapse of the western Roman Empire in the fifth century A.D. and the rise of Christianity, theatrically staged plays vanished as a form of entertainment for nearly a thousand years. Instructive religious dramas presented in the church as part of a mass slowly evolved into medieval mystery plays staged on church grounds. From the churchyard, these religious dramas moved to the marketplace and toured the countryside on wagons. It was not until the sixteenth century that drama broke entirely free of the church and set up, literally, on its own, largely because of the Renaissance interest in classical Roman and Greek theater. The first permanent indoor theater since the days of the Romans was designed by the Italian architect Palladio in Vincenza, Italy, in 1585. As a new theatrical space emerged from the canopy of the church, so did the characters presented in plays. Shakespeare, who belonged to the generation preceding Descartes', created characters who, occasionally, were so familiar with their new fictional world that they realized they were on stage. At the conclusion of *The Tempest*, a character addresses the audience and urges them to applaud the play they have just seen. Shakespeare not only created a new world but also populated it with citizens who sent messages back to the old.

Martin Luther, like his near contemporary Columbus, looked for a new route to an old place. Columbus, of course, wanted to find a shorter route to India. Luther wanted to sail completely around the Catholic Church and arrive, without an encumbering cargo of priests, at God. In 1517, Luther presented ninety-five theses against the church and offered to debate all comers. Following St. Paul, Luther held that salvation could be achieved only by faith in Jesus Christ. Thus, all the sacraments of the church, from baptism to priestly hierarchy, were excess baggage. Because salvation was strictly a matter of individual faith, the believer stood before God in a new land, beyond the controlling influence of Rome. Like Columbus, however, Luther may not have arrived where he intended. His pronouncement of a shorter, simpler route to the divine opened up centuries of religious warfare (which continue to this day in Northern Ireland) between Protestant and Catholic.

The development of astronomy in the sixteenth and seventeenth centuries is a literal example of the Renaissance exploration of new worlds. Until the advances of Tycho Brahe (1546–1601), Johannes Kepler (1571–1630), Nicolaus Copernicus (1473–1543), and Galileo (1564–1642), few had questioned that the universe was exactly as it appeared, a starry spectacle with the earth at its center. This geocentric view was supported not only by the testimony of the senses and Aristotle but also by the church. An earth-centered cosmology supported a God-centered philosophy and vice versa. So frightening was the new space discovered by the Renaissance astronomers that, so the story goes, when Galileo offered a priest a view through his new telescope, the churchman declined to look. Arrested by the Inquisition in 1633 and shown the instruments of his torture, Galileo decided the new universe wasn't out there and recanted his views.

Thus by Descartes' day, waves of Renaissance explorers had opened up new worlds, literary, artistic, theological, and astronomical. The new intellectual continents discovered by Luther and the astronomers were the most troublesome to the established order, and the church showed itself quite ready to burn rash explorers. Descartes understood his delicate task as dismounting the old views from their crumbling base and erecting them upon a new foundation.

DESCARTES' LIFE

René Descartes was born in 1596 at La Haye in Touraine, France. Having fragile health as a youth, he was allowed to sleep late in the day. Later in life, these long mornings became periods for philosophical reflection. Descartes attended La Fleche, a school run by the Jesuits, and studied philosophy and mathematics. Philosophy, as studied in Descartes' day, included the natural sciences as well as what we would think of as the more normal philosophical topics of logic (the study of the rules of reasoning), metaphysics (the study of the nature of reality), and ethics (the study of the nature of virtue). The young Descartes' intellectual skills were apparent to all.

The philosophical part of the curriculum at La Fleche was based upon the works of Aristotle and his Medieval commentators. Even though the revolutionary views of Galileo and Kepler had not penetrated the Jesuit school, Descartes' mathematical studies were up-to-date. He studied the geometry of the ancients and the algebra of the moderns (from the Arabs). The intellectual contradiction between Medieval philosophy, with its unquestioned assumptions about the universe, and the more rigorous "modern" mathematics may have laid the foundation for Descartes' search, later in life, for new, unquestionable certainties.

After his schooling, Descartes began an attempt to learn from, as he put it, "the book of the world." From age 22 to age 32, he traveled through the Netherlands, Poland, Bohemia, Austria, and Germany and served in two armies.

In 1622, Descartes sold his estates in France and used the proceeds to finance a new life in pursuit of Truth. He moved to Holland, a more philosophically liberal country than seventeenth-century France, and wrote *Rules for the Direction of the Mind,* his first sketch of his method of philosophy. Descartes openly asserted that the belief that the earth is the center of the cosmos was an ancient and vulgar falsehood. Five years later, Descartes finished *The World,* a discussion of the primary principles of all physics. He assumed a natural, not a divine, order for the celestial bodies. Descartes imagined God starting with matter endowed with nothing but the mathematical qualities of extension (three-dimensionality) and motion. As architect of the universe, God merely lent His aid to matter's proper distribution, organization, and continuation. God, in Descartes' view, became the watchmaker and the universe His divinely balanced watch. The only two spiritual, nonphysical substances were God and the human mind. Like Copernicus, Descartes asserted the movement of the earth. However, learning that the Inquisition had forced Galileo to recant his views supporting the Copernican theory, Descartes, a true son of the church and a cautious man, decided to withhold publication of *The World.*

In 1637, Descartes published *Discourse on Method,* an introduction to his philosophy and also a preface to his works in other sciences. He also published *La Geometrie,* which made an extremely important contribution to mathematics. His book linked algebra and geometry by means of a coordinate system that still bears his name: Cartesian. This system made Descartes one of the pioneers in the development of calculus.

At the age of 45, Descartes published *Meditations on First Philosophy.* In the *Meditations,* as you will soon learn, Descartes attempted to construct a universe of interrelated truths balanced upon a single, perfect certitude, his own existence as a "thinking thing."

In 1648, upset by local academic bickering and the possibility of physical harm by opponents of his works, Descartes accepted a position as tutor to Queen Christina of Sweden. Though Sweden promised a safe haven, he was not entirely eager to live in the land of "polar bears and ice."

Queen Christina, a remarkable woman, could speak five languages and rode and fenced as well as most men. She hired Descartes to teach her the "new philosophy"—that is, his own thinking. Ironically, teaching philosophy to someone who actually wanted to learn it caused Descartes' death. Christina insisted on meeting with him at five in the morning when her mind was clearest to do rigorous philosophical work. Descartes' lifelong habit had been to linger in bed until late. The demands of rising early each morning and the harsh weather of Stockholm weighed on him. On returning from a teaching session on an especially cold morning, Descartes contracted pneumonia; he died on February 11, 1650, at the age of 54.

One night of his life deserves special attention. On November 10, 1619, Descartes had three life-changing dreams. In one of those dreams, he heard a noise "like a thunderclap," which he thought was the Spirit of Truth descending upon him. The next morning, he was convinced the dreams foretold that he would develop a unifying method for philosophy and would establish the foundation of a "wonderful new science." He intended his new method to place philosophy firmly in the modern world of new sciences and free it from its reliance on ancient authority.

THE OLD IN DESCARTES' PHILOSOPHY

The two major philosophical periods before Descartes and the Renaissance were the Medieval and the Classical. Despite his intention to begin a "wonderful new science," important aspects of his philosophy can be found in thinkers before his time. Descartes himself points out that his arguments against certitude in *Meditation I* are not new and can be traced back to the Classical philosopher Sextus Empiricus. (You will see how he attempts to refute these skeptical arguments in *Meditations II–VI.*) Another influence on Descartes was the Classical Greek philosopher Plato (fifth to fourth century B.C.). Descartes uses Plato's concept of the relationship between the perfect and the imperfect to prove God's existence. In dialogues like the *Phaedo, Symposium,* and *Republic,* Plato essentially argued that whenever we make a judgment, such as "This is not a perfectly beautiful painting," the implication is that we have an idea about what Perfect Beauty actually is, if only in a dim way. Just as our idea of a foot ruler can be traced back to our actual experience of a foot ruler, our idea of Perfect Beauty can be traced back to our actual experience with Perfect Beauty (in Plato's argument, to a time before our birth). We can reason that Perfect Beauty exists every time we use knowledge of it to judge that something is not perfectly beautiful.

Now think for a few moments, reread the previous paragraph, and try to say in your own words what I just said about Plato.

What you seem to be saying about Plato is _____

_____ .

You offered the example of a foot ruler. My example of the point

Plato is making is _____

_____ . The way

this applies to Plato's argument about Perfect Beauty is _____

_____

_____ .

Descartes adapts Plato's idea to a proof of God's existence. Descartes knows he is an imperfect being. But this implies that he also knows what a perfect being is. The idea of a perfect being could have come only from a real perfect being. Therefore, whereas Plato concludes that Perfect Beauty exists, Descartes concludes that the perfect being, God, exists. (We will talk more about this proof later on the tour.)

This God of Descartes, however, is the God of Medieval Christian philosophers. Descartes agrees with his Medieval predecessors that God is his creator. Descartes continues the tradition of Medieval philosophy that God left His stamp on Descartes' mind much as a potter leaves his mark on his pot. Echoing many prayers from the Middle Ages, Descartes contemplates this God in wonder and delight at the end of *Meditation III*. The agency of this God, the centuries-old Catholic Church and its powerful supporters, are to be courted, as Descartes does in his prefatory letter to the *Meditations* (not included in this edition). Descartes' connection of God's existence to His essence is first clearly stated by Anselm (eleventh century A.D.) in his *Proslogium*, and Descartes' problem with the existence of error in a creation by a perfect God also worried Augustine (fifth century A.D.) in his *Confessions*. Now try summing this up.

What Descartes owes to Plato is _____

_____

_____ . The way he applies this to a

proof of God's existence is _____

_____

_____ . Some ideas and concerns he

borrows from Medieval philosophers are _____

_____ .

THE NEW IN DESCARTES' PHILOSOPHY

Several new aspects of Descartes' philosophy qualify him as the "father of modern philosophy."

In *Meditation II*, Descartes analyzes a piece of wax and distinguishes between what is learned about the wax through the senses and what is learned by the mind. In the process, he develops a new definition of the essential characteristics of a body. Because the color, shape, smell, and solidity of the wax change when it becomes warm, none of those things can be part of its essential character. The wax is still wax whether it is hard or soft, bright or dull, sweet smelling or scentless. Descartes argues that all these changing characteristics come to us through our senses, and therefore our senses do not tell us about the unchanging, essential characteristics of the wax. Only inspection by our minds reveals that wax, and therefore all other bodies, are in essence spatially extended, flexible, and capable of changing form. This nonsensory definition of matter will eventually lead to Newton's mathematical description of matter in the eighteenth century.

Descartes thus argues that the mind is one thing and the senses are another. What the mind knows for certain did not come from the senses. In fact, all through the *Meditations*, Descartes describes the mind as completely separable from the body. Such a sharp distinction between mind and body has been labeled "Cartesian dualism" and has been an important legacy to the history of psychology. In one sense, Descartes' journey inward into the privacy of his own mind makes possible Freud's psychoanalytic self-examination at the beginning of the twentieth century.

Descartes shares his Medieval predecessors' concern with God's existence, but unlike the proofs of others before him, his proof of God's existence depends on his prior proof of his own existence. This is an important shift. When Anselm demonstrates God's existence, he does it in the context of a long prayer, the *Proslogium* (see Appendix A). Anselm is dissatisfied with his proof when it doesn't make him feel closer to God. When Descartes uses similar arguments, he does it in the context of a meditation designed to make him feel more sure of his own conclusions. Anselm's proof draws him upward to God; Descartes' proof is subsumed by a larger and more important project, his own philosophical peace of mind.

Descartes almost never quotes anyone. One Medieval proof of the truth of an argument is to show that the Bible, or Aristotle, or someone who lived long ago stated the same thing. Thus, to be true is to be consistent with the wisdom of the past. Descartes is suspicious even of his own past. In *Meditation I*, he deliberately sets himself adrift from all his past beliefs. In *Meditation III*, he questions what he established in *Meditation II*. In *Meditation IV*, he has to review again what he said in *Meditation III*. Not only does he find no comfort in a truth that someone wise held to be true long ago, but also he finds no comfort in a truth he held to be true moments ago. The past, even his own past, is always to be viewed with suspicion.

Augustine, Anselm, and Aquinas, Descartes' three great Medieval predecessors, spent a great amount of time explaining the relationship between a perfect God and an imperfect creation. If we place too great an emphasis on God's perfection, an unbridgeable chasm opens between the divine and the created. Thus, the problem for Medieval philosophy is simultaneously to demonstrate the absolute chasm between the universe and God and to define some bridge (grace, Christ, reason, faith?) across that chasm. Descartes, a Renaissance philosopher, spends a great amount of time trying to get out of his own head. It is not so much the disorder of the universe that troubles him as the disorder of his own thoughts. The chasm Descartes is worried about is between his thought and its object. He does not think about the universe and God as much as he thinks about his own thinking about the universe and God.

What are some of the new aspects of Descartes' philosophy? (You've already noted that a tour in philosophy means you go forward only to go back. Or, to put it in a more positive light, you go back to go forward.)

The points that are new in Descartes are _____

_____

_____

_____ .

A SUMMARY OF THE MEDITATIONS

In *Meditation I,* Descartes begins to ask the fundamental question for his thought: Is there anything of which I can be certain? In his quest for certainty, Descartes vows to doubt all his former opinions. If there are grounds for doubting them, they cannot be completely certain. Descartes is searching for a foundation, for solid rock underneath the shifting soils of his world. He doubts his senses and even has a difficult time distinguishing dreaming from reality. (This is interesting in light of his earlier dream.) At this point, he finds no certain method for telling dreams from waking experience. He imagines there is an evil spirit, a great deceiver, who misleads him on every possible occasion. If he can find a truth even an all-powerful evil spirit could not deceive him about, he will have found an initial 100 percent certitude. *Meditation I* ends with nothing certain except that nothing appears certain.

Meditation II rescues the project of doubt from absolute skepticism by the famous argument that the one idea that cannot be doubted is that "*I am doubting.*" As I doubt, I can doubt everything except that I must exist in order to doubt that I exist. " 'I am, I exist' must be true whenever I state it or mentally consider it." But what or who is this "I"? For Descartes, the "I" is a thing that thinks. Descartes has a "clear and distinct" idea of the mind (soul) in a way that there is no clear and distinct idea of the body. At the end of *Meditation II,* Descartes is able to say, "For so far I do not admit in myself anything other than the mind." So Descartes begins a process of methodological doubting and can doubt everything except the self, the mind, the "I" that doubts.

Meditation III takes as one of its tasks the demonstration of the existence of God. It is important to remember the direction of Descartes' thought here: From the certainty of the self comes the certainty of God. That is new. Briefly, one of his arguments is that the idea of a supremely perfect being comes from a supremely perfect cause (God). Something that is more perfect (the idea of God) cannot be produced by something that is less perfect (Descartes' mind); therefore, God exists because He is the only possible cause of Descartes' idea of Him. In the second proof, Descartes argues that God must exist in order to guarantee Descartes' continued existence. Since Descartes cannot be the continuous cause of his own existence, God must be that cause and therefore God must exist.

Meditation IV continues with a description of the characteristics of God and begins to explore questions about truth and error. God, whose existence Descartes just proved, cannot be a deceiver. A God who deceived would not be perfect, that is, would not be God. But if God cannot deceive, where do errors and mistakes come from? Descartes says that error is a function of the incorrect application of will to the objects of the understanding. We can will to do more than we can immediately, correctly understand. Nonetheless, he goes on to assert that those things that we perceive *clearly and distinctly* are true. Descartes' quest for certainty is now a function of finding the clear and distinct.

Meditation V offers an additional proof of the existence of God and begins to consider the reality of the sensible world that he has been doubting so vigorously throughout the previous Meditations. In his proof, Descartes argues that just as it is impossible to conceive of a mountain range without valleys, he cannot conceive of God except as existing. God is to His existence as a mountain range is to mountain valleys; wherever you have one, you necessarily have the other. God has all perfections, one perfection is existence, therefore God must exist. (This is similar to the ontological argument used several hundred years before Descartes by Anselm. See Appendix A.) Having once again demonstrated the existence of God, Descartes can affirm all knowledge of clear and distinct ideas, even knowledge, in principle, of the world. God, who created him, would be a deceiver if Descartes' clear and distinct ideas about the world were false. Once the self is certain, God is certain, and the existence of the world and material objects can be, at least in principle, saved from Descartes' original project of doubt.

Meditation VI deals with the existence of physical things and the distinction between the mind and the body. Since God is not a deceiver and since there must be some cause of the ideas of physical reality, "it follows that physical objects exist." To a twentieth-century philosopher, accustomed to thinking in a different fashion, this assertion might seem obvious. But for Descartes, *Meditation VI* has redeemed the reality of the self, of God, and of the world. Given one firm standpoint, his own existence, Descartes has saved his world from destruction by his doubt.

THINKING LIKE DESCARTES

In the work you are about to read, Descartes takes his world apart and then puts it back together. He begins by wondering what he can know for certain. To begin to understand his philosophical method, make five statements you are fairly certain are true.

1. _My father is Srikant Raghavan_
2. _I am a human being_.
3. _I am 20 yrs old_.
4. _I am from India_.
5. _The earth is round_.

Of the five statements you just made, which two of the five would be easiest for you to doubt?

The one I could doubt the easiest would be number _____

because it is possible that _____ .

I might be able to doubt number _____ because it is possible

that _____ .

You would certainly admit there are degrees of certitude. How certain are you about the weather tomorrow?

I am _____ percent certain that tomorrow it will be _____

_____ .

Now try for several higher levels of certainty about some other truths.

I am _____ percent certain that _____ .

And I am still more certain that _____ .

Of that I am _____ percent certain!

How convinced are you that triangles have three sides?

I am _____ percent certain.

And which of your five statements seems as certain to you as the truth that triangles have three sides?

I am _____ percent certain that _____

because _____

_____ .

You have just begun to practice thinking like Descartes. You began by thinking about things you believed were true. You doubted the complete certitude of two of them. You began to see that you could be more certain of some truths than others. You found a standard of certitude (a truth you could know as certain as the truth that triangles have three sides). You used that standard to establish a single 100 percent certitude. Descartes does much the same thing. In *Meditation I*, he starts by looking for absolute truths. He proposes and rejects, for interesting reasons, whole categories of beliefs. He ends the Meditation with a wonderful test of 100 percent certitude. In the succeeding Meditations, he begins carefully to chain together truths he can be completely positive about. At every stage, he raises counterarguments against himself and then refutes those counterarguments. In essence, he believes he can be 100 percent certain that he exists, then that God exists, then that any idea he can perceive of "clearly and distinctly" is true, then that he is led into error only because he incorrectly combines will and understanding, then that the principles of mathematics are true, and finally that the material world exists.

Just as one of the best ways to appreciate a sport is to play it yourself, one of the best ways to understand philosophy is to try solving philosophical problems yourself. Descartes, in *Meditation III*, proves that God exists. Try it. And then practice thinking like Descartes by arguing strongly against your own proof. And then, truly imitating Descartes, try to refute your own refutation.

God is a being who _____ .
Now I need to link together several obvious truths and then deduce from these truths that God exists. First, it is a fact that

_____ because

_____ .

Second, it is a fact that _____

because _____ .

The other facts I need to establish, with a reason for each are:

_____ .

_____ .

_____ .

_____ .

From all this it follows that God exists because _____

_____ .

Looking back at my argument, I see that the weakest link is step

number _____

because _____

_____ . But I can disprove what I

just saying _____

_____ .

Having said all that, I am _____ percent certain that God exists

and _____ percent certain that my proof cannot be doubted by any reasonable person.

If you didn't give yourself 100 percent on the last two points, you don't measure up to Descartes' confidence. You will have numerous chances later on the tour to practice thinking like Descartes.

YOUR PHILOSOPHICAL SELF-PORTRAIT

Sketch your philosophical self-portrait by answering the questions below and offering evidence for your answers.

1. T F   Very little, if anything, can be known for certain.

    Evidence: _____

    _____

    _____ .

2. T F   From the fact that you are a thinking being, it is possible to prove that you exist.

    Evidence: _____

    _____

    _____ .

3. T F   From the fact that you exist, it is possible to prove that you are a thinking being.

    Evidence: _____

    _____

    _____ .

4. T F   It is possible, without using knowledge gained by the senses, to prove that God exists.

    Evidence: _____

    _____

    _____ .

5. T   F   You could not have the idea of a perfect being (God) unless an actual perfect being (God) existed.

Evidence: _____

_____

_____ .

When you are finished with the *Meditations*, compare your position to Descartes' on page 96.

READING DESCARTES

Reading anything written long ago is like time travel. Reading Descartes may be as initially confusing as if you found yourself in his seventeenth-century Paris. In the following *Meditations on First Philosophy,* you are thrust into the middle of a world, a way of thinking, and a set of mental customs that are alien to you. This tour was designed to help you find your way around.

Let me get you off to a good start by guiding you very slowly through the first paragraph.

Here is the first sentence:

"For several years now, I've been aware that I accepted many falsehoods as true in my youth, that what I built on the foundation of these falsehoods was dubious, and accordingly that once in my life I would need to tear down everything and begin anew from the foundations if I wanted to establish any stable and lasting knowledge."

What do you think that means?

He is saying _____

_____ .

Now, let's look more closely at this long sentence. The best strategy in analyzing long sentences is to look at the clauses separated by commas and concentrate on the meaning of each of the units. For example:

"For several years now, I've been aware that I accepted many falsehoods as true in my youth . . ."

That much, standing alone, is not terribly difficult to understand. What happened in his youth?

He _____

_____ .

Now add the next clause to it.

"For several years now, I've been aware that I accepted many falsehoods as true in my youth, **that what I built on the foundation of these falsehoods was dubious . . ."**

He is describing a progression. First something happened in his youth and then something else happened.

He is saying _____

_____ .

Now add the rest of the sentence, and see what the conclusion of the progression is.

"For several years now, I've been aware that I accepted many falsehoods as true in my youth, that what I built on the foundation of these falsehoods was dubious, **and accordingly that once in my life I would need to tear down everything and begin anew from the foundations if I wanted to establish any stable and lasting knowledge.**"

The first sentence is crucial because it states Descartes' problem and what he will have to do to solve it. The section in boldface above presents his proposed solution.

His problem is _____ .

His solution is _____ .

At this point, you probably understand the first sentence better than when you first read it. Here is the rest of the first paragraph. Reread it several times, break sentences into smaller, more understandable pieces, make your own notes in the margin, underline important points.

"But the task seemed enormous, and I waited until I was so old that no better time for undertaking it would be likely to follow. I have thus delayed so long that it would be wrong for me to waste in indecision the time left for action. Today, then, having rid myself of worries and having arranged for some peace and quiet, I withdraw alone, free at last earnestly and wholeheartedly to overthrow all my beliefs."

Now, try to paraphrase each sentence.

In the first sentence, he is saying _____

_____ .

In the second sentence, he is saying _____

_____ .

In the third sentence, he is saying _____

_____ .

Now what, in essence, is the first paragraph about?

What he is going to do is _____

because _____ .

One thing you may already realize is that the reading pattern for understanding philosophy is different from your normal reading pattern. Usually you read in a straight line. You begin at the beginning and go on to the end. Reading most philosophy in that fashion is simply impossible. You must circle back, stop, reflect, translate ideas into your own words in the margin, underline, go back again, and then move slowly forward. This tour will guide you through most of the steps you need to take. In addition, add your own careful underlining and margin notes. If you are not sure what to write in the margins, just try to answer this question over and over: "What is the general idea of this paragraph?" Put question marks in the margins where you are confused.

Besides the occasional complexity of Descartes' sentences, his philosophical method may cause you difficulty. Before I began to read philosophy, I imagined that philosophical thinking was something one did when one couldn't sleep, and it went something like this:

"The universe is such a big place. I am so small. Where does the universe end? If I went way out into space and came to the end of the universe, what would be beyond that? Something? Nothing? What am I thinking about?"

By *philosophical* I meant anything that seemed big and confusing. You are about to discover what Descartes means by philosophical thinking. Whereas my questions led me to greater confusion, his lead him to greater clarity. Draw a line across the page wherever he seems to begin an important new question. Sometimes he questions his own answers. Read very slowly at these points. Part of his method is to say things he eventually decides are false. There are some excellent examples of this in *Meditation I.* I'll point them out when they occur.

Now think back over what I have said to begin your tour, and make whatever notes you need to guide you on your way.

When I think back over these opening pages, I want to remember

_____

_____

_____

_____ .

TRANSLATOR'S PREFACE

This preface and the accompanying translation of the Meditations *first appeared in* Rene Descartes's Meditations on First Philosophy, *trans. Ronald Rubin (Claremont: Areté Press, 1986). They are used here with the permission of the translator and of the original publisher.*

The Latin in which the *Meditations* (1641) were written did not seem strange or old-fashioned to its seventeenth-century audience, and I therefore don't see why the English into which they're translated should seem odd to their modern readers. So, I have tried to translate the *Meditations* into straightforward English prose—even where that has meant departing somewhat from the diction or syntax of Descartes' Latin. I hope that, in this way, I have increased the likelihood of readers' viewing the *Meditations* as the report of a living philosophical project.

In a work other than the *Meditations* (namely, his *Reply to Bourdin*), Descartes describes this project with a simple metaphor. If we suspect that some of the apples in a barrel are rotten (he says), we should dump them all out, look at them one by one, and replace the ones that are flawless. Accordingly, after noting that his beliefs can be called into doubt, Descartes resolves to rid himself of all his opinions and to reeducate himself from scratch (*Meditation I*)! The first belief that he "puts back into the barrel" is that he himself exists (*Meditation II*). And, from this single point, he attempts to establish with certainty that God exists (*Meditations III* and *V*), that we can be absolutely certain of the truth of what we grasp "clearly and distinctly" (*Meditations IV* and *V*), that the physical world exists (*Meditation VI*), and that his mind is distinct from his body (*Meditation VI*).

For the most part, I offer the translation of the *Meditations* without notes or comments. I will say something, however, about the peculiar phrases that begin to appear around the middle of *Meditation III*—phrases like "subjective reality," "formal reality," "eminent reality," "degree of reality," "substance," and "nature." Descartes seems to have assumed that his readers would be familiar with these terms before opening the *Meditations*, but few today are familiar with the philosophic picture from which they get their meanings.

According to this picture, there are different *degrees* of reality and different *kinds* of reality as well. This sounds strange because we tend to think that something is either completely real or completely unreal—that there is no middle ground between existence and nonexistence. But Descartes thought differently.

As he saw it, the closer a thing is to being a substance (that is, a thing that can exist on its own), the higher its degree of reality. Thus, a fender has a higher degree of reality than a dent in the fender, since the fender can exist more or less on its own while the dent cannot possibly exist without the fender. Similarly, if things like fenders derive their existence moment by moment from God (as Descartes suggests near the end of *Meditation III*), God has a higher degree of reality than such things.

Now compare the dent in the fender to, say, Sherlock Holmes. Since Holmes is a substance while the dent is something that must exist in a substance, Holmes has higher degree of reality than the dent. Still, there's a point to saying that the dent is *more* real than Holmes: While the dent is something that we can actually see and touch, Holmes is entirely fictional. To mark this difference, Descartes distinguishes subjective reality (*objectiva realitas*, in Latin) from formal reality (*formalis realitas*). Things that are the object of someone's thought are said to have subjective reality, while things that *we* would say "*really* exist" are said to have formal reality. Thus, the dent in the car's fender and the fender itself both have formal reality (and subjective reality, too, when someone thinks of them), but Holmes merely has subjective reality. (The reality of God—namely, eminent reality—is supposed to stand to formal reality roughly as formal reality stands to subjective reality.)

The distinction of subjective reality from formal reality is connected to a view about *natures*. As Descartes sees it, a nature can exist either subjectively or formally. Consider, for instance, the nature of the sun. When Descartes regards this nature as having subjective reality (that is, when he thinks of its appearing before someone's mind as an object of thought), he calls it *the idea of the sun*. But, when he regards the very same nature as having formal reality, he simply calls it *the sun*. So, according to Descartes, "the idea of the sun is the sun itself existing in the understanding, not formally as it does in the sky, but subjectively— that is, as things normally exist in the understanding" *(Reply to Caterus)*. The passages in which Descartes seems to say that he *is* a thinking *nature* therefore should not be written off as slips of his pen (or of mine!). On Descartes' theory, an existing mind *is* a nature—a thinking nature with formal reality. And, similarly, an existing physical object is a nature—a material nature with formal reality.

One final point about the translation: While it's usual to translate the Latin verb "*imaginari*" with "to imagine," I've often translated it with a phrase like "to have a mental image." In English, the verb "to imagine" can simply mean "to suppose." But, when Descartes used the verb "*imaginari*," he's talking about picturing a thing in the mind as if looking at it, not just about pretending or supposing that it exists.

With the exceptions that I have mentioned, I've tried to use the expressions in the translation in their usual, nontechnical senses.

Ronald Rubin
Claremont, California

MEDITATION I

⌘

On What Can Be Called
Into Doubt

PREVIEW

Searching for a truth that cannot be doubted, Descartes tears his beliefs down to their foundations. He discovers that nothing certain comes to him through his senses and that he cannot tell dreaming from waking. If Descartes cannot prove that God is no deceiver, then he cannot know even the simplest mathematical truths. To guard against returning to his former misplaced confidence in his beliefs, Descartes concludes *Meditation I* by imagining an evil demon, "supremely powerful and cunning, who works as hard as he can to deceive me."

Note the special way Descartes argues with himself. He believes he cannot know anything for certain unless he argues as strongly as he can against certitude. Label the arguments *Pro* that support certainty; label the arguments *Con* that attack certainty. *Pro* arguments take Descartes closer to his goal of perfect knowledge; *Con* arguments take him farther away.

MEDITATION I

Some falsehoods, such as the existence of Santa Claus, that you accepted as true in your youth are

_____

_____

_____

_____ .

Instead of refuting each of his beliefs individually, Descartes decides to

_____

_____

_____ .

For several years now, I've been aware that I accepted many falsehoods as true in my youth, that what I built on the foundation of those falsehoods was dubious, and accordingly that once in my life I would need to tear down everything and begin anew from the foundations if I wanted to establish any stable and lasting knowledge. But the task seemed enormous, and I waited until I was so old that no better time for undertaking it would be likely to follow. I have thus delayed so long that it would be wrong for me to waste in indecision the time left for action. Today, then, having rid myself of worries and having arranged for some peace and quiet, I withdraw alone, free at last earnestly and wholeheartedly to overthrow all my beliefs.

To do this, I don't need to show each of them to be false; I may never be able to do that. But, since reason now convinces me that I ought to withhold my assent just as carefully from what isn't obviously certain and indubitable as from what's obviously false, I can justify the rejection of all my beliefs if in each I can find some ground for doubt. And, to do this, I need not run through my beliefs one by one, which would be an endless task. Since a building collapses when its foundation is cut out from under it, I will go straight to the principles on which all my former beliefs rested.

Of course, whatever I have so far accepted as supremely true I have learned either from the senses or through the senses. But I have occasionally caught the senses deceiving me, and it's prudent never completely to trust those who have cheated us even once.

But, while my senses may deceive me about what is small or far away, there may still be other things that I take in by the senses but that I cannot possibly doubt—like that I am here, sitting before the fire, wearing a dressing gown, touching this paper. And on what grounds might I deny that my hands and the other parts of my body exist?—unless perhaps I liken myself to madmen whose brains are so rattled by the persistent vapors of melancholy that they are sure that they're kings when in fact they are paupers, or that they wear purple robes when in fact they're naked, or that their heads are clay, or that they are gourds, or made of glass. But these people are insane, and I would seem just as crazy if I were to apply what I say about them to myself.

This would be perfectly obvious—if I weren't a man accustomed to sleeping at night whose experiences while asleep are at least as far-fetched as those that madmen have while awake. How often, at night, I've been convinced that I was here, sitting before the fire, wearing my dressing gown, when in fact I was undressed and between the covers of my bed! But now I am looking at this piece of paper with my eyes wide open; the head that I am shaking has not been lulled to sleep; I put my hand out consciously and deliberately and feel. None of this would be as distinct if I were asleep. As if I can't remember having been tricked by similar thoughts while asleep! When I think very carefully about this, I see so plainly that there are no reliable signs by which I can distinguish sleeping from waking that I am stupefied—and my stupor itself suggests that I am asleep!

Suppose, then, that I am dreaming. Suppose, in particular, that my eyes are not open, that my head is not moving, and that I have not put out my hand. Suppose that I do not have hands, or even a body. I must still admit that the things I see in sleep are like painted images which must have been patterned after real things and, hence, that things like eyes, heads, hands, and bodies are real rather than imaginary. For, even when painters try to give bizarre shapes to sirens and satyrs, they are unable to give them completely new natures; they only jumble together the parts of various animals. And, even if they were to come up with something so novel that no one had ever seen anything like it before, something entirely fictitious and unreal, at least there must be real colors from which they composed it. Similarly, while things like eyes, heads, and hands may be imaginary, it must be granted that some simpler and more universal things are real—the "real colors" from which the true and false images in our thoughts are formed.

Things of this sort seem to include general bodily nature and its extension, the shape of extended things, their quantity (that is, their size and number), the place in which they exist, the time through which they endure and so on.

Perhaps we can correctly infer that, while physics, astronomy, medicine, and other disciplines that require the study of composites are dubious, disciplines like arithmetic and geometry, which deal only with completely

Circle the word "but" whenever it introduces a new *Pro* or *Con* argument.

Descartes has decided that although his senses may be wrong about

_____

_____ ,

they could not be wrong about

_____

_____

_____ .

In this paragraph, Descartes changes his mind about _____

_____

_____

because _____

_____

_____ .

Even if he is dreaming, Descartes now decides that he can be certain

about _____

_____

_____

_____ .

Reread this and the previous two paragraphs. The stages Descartes has already gone through are

_____

_____

_____

_____

_____ .

Geometry is more certain than

astronomy because _____

_____

_____

_____ .

"Nevertheless," "Maybe," and "But" are the first words of this paragraph and the next two paragraphs. Throughout the six Meditations, circle key words like these to show where the argument is moving in a new direction.

means to an end? learning experience?

"These views" refers to _____

_____

_____

_____ .

This is one of the most famous paragraphs in the *Meditations*. The advantage to Descartes of supposing "an evil demon" exists who is

deceiving him is _____

_____

_____

_____ .

simple and universal things without regard to whether they exist in the world, are somehow certain and indubitable. For, whether we are awake or asleep, two plus three is always five, and the square never has more than four sides. It seems impossible even to suspect such obvious truths of falsity.

Nevertheless, the traditional view is fixed in my mind that there is a God who can do anything and by whom I have been made to be as I am. How do I know that He hasn't brought it about that, while there is in fact no earth, no sky, no extended thing, no shape, no magnitude, and no place, all of these things seem to me to exist, just as they do now? I think that other people sometimes err in what they believe themselves to know perfectly well. Mightn't I be deceived when I add two and three, or count the sides of a square, or do even simpler things, if we can even suppose that there is anything simpler? Maybe it will be denied that God deceives me, since He is said to be supremely good. But, if God's being good is incompatible with His having created me so that I am deceived always, it seems just as out of line with His being good that He permits me to be deceived sometimes—as he undeniably does.

Maybe some would rather deny that there is an omnipotent God than believe that everything else is uncertain. Rather than arguing with them, I will grant everything I have said about God to be fiction. But, however these people think I came to be as I now am—whether they say it is by fate, or by accident, or by a continuous series of events, or in some other way—it seems that he who errs and is deceived is somehow imperfect. Hence, the less power that is attributed to my original creator, the more likely it is that I am always deceived. To these arguments, I have no reply. I'm forced to admit that nothing that I used to believe is beyond legitimate doubt—not because I have been careless or playful, but because I have valid and well-considered grounds for doubt. Hence, I must withhold my assent from my former beliefs as carefully as from obvious falsehoods if I want to arrive at something certain.

But it's not enough to have noticed this: I must also take care to bear it in mind. For my habitual views constantly return to my mind and take control of what I believe as if our long-standing, intimate relationship has given them the right to do so, even against my will. I'll never break the habit of trusting and giving in to these views while I see them for what they are—things somewhat dubious (as I have just shown) but nonetheless probable, things that I have much more reason to believe than to deny. That's why I think it will be good deliberately to turn my will around, to allow myself to be deceived, and to suppose that all my previous beliefs are false and illusory. Eventually, when I have counterbalanced the weight of my prejudices, my bad habits will no longer distort my grasp of things. I know that there is no danger of error here and that I won't overindulge in skepticism, since I'm now concerned, not with action, but only with gaining knowledge.

I will suppose, then, not that there is a supremely good God who is the source of all truth, but that there is an evil demon, supremely powerful and cunning, who works as hard as he can to deceive me. I will say that sky, air, earth, color, shape, sound, and other external things are just dreamed illusions that the demon uses to ensnare my judgment. I will regard myself as not having hands, eyes, flesh, blood, and senses—but as having the false belief that I have all these things. I will obstinately concentrate on this meditation and will thus ensure by mental resolution that, if I do not really have the ability to know the truth, I will at least withhold assent from what is false and from what a deceiver may try to put over on me, however powerful and cunning he may be. But this plan requires effort, and laziness brings me back to my ordinary life. I am like a prisoner who happens to enjoy the illusion of freedom in his dreams, begins to suspect that he is asleep, fears being awakened, and deliberately lets the enticing illusions skip by unchallenged. Thus, I slide back into my old views, afraid to awaken and to find that after my peaceful rest I must toil, not in the light, but in the confusing darkness of the problems just raised.

The main "problems just raised" are

_____

_____

_____

_____

_____

_____

_____.

LEARNING PHILOSOPHY FROM DESCARTES

The most common question my students ask about the *Meditations* is simply "Why is Descartes doing this?"

Descartes appears to be troubling himself with doubts about issues that don't seem doubtful. Knowledge, despite what Descartes says in *Meditation I*, certainly seems to come through the senses. Therefore, my students ask, why should a philosopher go back and forth through complex arguments wondering about something that is so obvious?

Right now, you might say, you are getting knowledge about Descartes by reading this book. Your eyes scan the page; your brain processes the information. Therefore, you might justifiably wonder, why isn't the way the mind and the senses work just as obvious to Descartes? Why doesn't he just conclude that "all my beliefs rest on data that have come to me through my senses and that my mind organizes; thus, my beliefs have a sturdy foundation"? End of meditation.

Many students want to take their objections about Descartes even further and attack philosophy in general. Why on earth do philosophers worry about all the problems they worry about? Their reasonings are just mind games. Anyone can tell reality from illusion, right from wrong, fact from error. No one needs an impossible-to-understand, philosophical manuscript as a guidebook to daily life.

Thus, Descartes seems to be just another egghead making simple things complex. The *Meditations* are fancy talk about the obvious. Philosophers are dogs worrying a meatless bone. The world is the world. Knowledge is knowledge. The true is the true and the false is the false. And that is that.

I hope it surprises you when I say that, with one exception, I agree. I have spent 99 percent of my life not worried in the slightest about Descartes' problems. I sit in chairs and never wonder if I am dreaming I'm sitting there. These are my hands, and two plus three is certainly five. God has better things to do than deceive me about such obvious truths. Except on the occasion I will soon describe, I keep my evil demon locked up.

Just like you, I trust my senses. It is too much trouble not to. If I had to think about whether or not my fingers were touching the computer keyboard right now and whether or not pushing down each key would put "real" information on the screen and whether or not your senses would work accurately when you read these black squiggles, I'd never write a word. In the same way, I imagine, a physicist doesn't wonder if, because matter is mostly empty space, her cup will fall through the table when she sets it down. Nor does she worry that because there is a discontinuity between quantum theory and celestial mechanics, her dinner might cook improperly.

Our unexamined beliefs about daily life do very well in guiding us through the world we live in. We don't need to understand the nature of truth to use the microwave.

So why bother with Descartes?

As I said earlier, I bother with Descartes only on one kind of occasion. The rest of my hours, I can do without him.

As long as I attend to the small mysteries of life, Descartes is useless. A thousand questions stream at me every day and I do not appeal to what I know about Descartes for help. Is it cold enough to wear a coat? Should I have hamburger again tonight? Will my darling get angry if I refuse to watch *The Sound of Music*? On these and many other occasions, Descartes is mute and irrelevant.

I turn to Descartes, and philosophy, for guidance only when I lift my eyes from life's small mysteries to its Great Mysteries. To put this paradoxically, philosophy is rarely important and therefore very important.

Does God exist? Where did the Universe come from? Do I have a soul? When I confront these questions, everything I have learned about the weather for coats, the tastiness of repeated meals of hamburger, and the moods of my darling becomes irrelevant. Only Descartes (and other philosophers) shows me how to think about the Great Mysteries. In fact, I cannot very usefully confront any of the Great Mysteries on my own. Because I spend 99 percent of my time not thinking about such things, I have no clue to how to think about life's biggest questions. There is the Universe. How do I think about it? It's big. It's starry. And? I must turn to philosophy to see how great minds have considered the question. When I want to contemplate the workings of the cosmos, I need those whom the centuries have selected as the wisest guides. On the rare occasions when I get my head above the clouds, I do well to lay against the starry sky templates of genius.

And so, why is Descartes doing what he is doing? Is it a fair criticism to argue that he does not address life's daily problems, that his writings are hard to understand, and that he makes the simple complex?

What's philosophy about anyway?

It is no good criticizing philosophy because it does not address life's daily problems, just as it would be no good criticizing an astronomical telescope because it does not help you watch TV. Philosophy is a big-view kind of thing. Stay away from it when you're looking for mild entertainment. But, also, don't criticize philosophy for not being a small-view kind of thing. The globe is not useless because it doesn't help you find the shortest route to work.

Nor is it any good criticizing philosophy for being difficult to understand. You and I spend most of our lives among life's small mysteries. We are, by nature and habit, small, unsystematic thinkers.

Philosophy requires that we think grandly and carefully. Among other strange mental practices, philosophy asks us to think about thinking. This is rather like putting your toe behind your ear. Of course it hurts. The toe has voyaged into the land of nonordinary toeness. So your mind will hurt after reading philosophy. Everyone's does. Philosophy cramps the mind into unnatural contortions. But its promise is enlightenment.

This needs to be stressed. Philosophy promises enlightenment. Why do we twist our minds into unnatural philosophical contortions? Because philosophy promises true answers to the Great Mysteries! In these *Meditations,* Descartes will establish all that can be known for certain, prove God's existence three ways, describe the nature of the mind, show a way to avoid all error, destroy every basis for doubt, and construct a world of certitude. That's worth at least stretching your toe in the direction of your ear.

Finally, it is no good criticizing philosophy for making the simple complex. Actually, philosophy shows the complexity of the simple. Think, for a second, about washing machines. You would certainly say that a washing machine is less complex than all of reality. And yet, a washing machine is mystery enough to confound most consumers. There are thick manuals that do nothing but explain the workings of the workings of washing machines. Certainly the interactions of the mind and the cosmos are more complex than devices that force soapy water through our clothes. If washing machines are not simple, then certainly neither are the mind and the nature of reality. And if we grant that our home appliances are very complicated and need specialists (such as washing machine repair people) for their analysis, then we also ought to grant that the workings of reality need specialists (such as philosophers) for its analysis. And just as we would not expect to be able to follow the reasonings in a washing repair manual at first glance, so we should not expect to follow the reasonings of a philosophical meditation at first glance.

Where does this leave you? One-sixth of the way through an exploration of a great philosophical exploration. Take heart. Philosophy is difficult because it is a nonordinary (perhaps someday you will say an extraordinary) kind of thinking; philosophy is useless for life's small mysteries because it is a tool designed for life's Great Mysteries; and philosophy is hard to comprehend because it is a specialized kind of knowledge you are unfamiliar with.

Philosophy is a toe-behind-the-ear sort of thing that promises enlightenment.

THINKING ABOUT MEDITATION I

Look back at your underlinings and margin notes and try to say in a general way what *Meditation I* is about.

What Descartes is seeking is _____

_____ . The major points he establishes after the

opening are _____

_____

_____ .

Let's consider a few sections more carefully. In the Introduction, we analyzed the first paragraph. Descartes concludes that paragraph by saying he wants "to overthrow all my beliefs." Once more, why does he want to do that?

Because _____

_____ .

Descartes then goes on to criticize knowledge gained through his senses. But, even though his senses occasionally mislead him, he believes he would be like a madman if he doubted something so obvious as that he is "sitting before the fire, wearing a dressing gown, touching this paper." Start by thinking about some specific occasions when you were fooled by your senses.

One time I thought I saw _____ , but I was wrong because

_____ . Or I thought

I heard _____ , but what was really

happening was _____ . But even though my senses do sometimes deceive me, it would seem insane to say they are doing so when they tell me I am reading this book.

I almost agree, but read the following passage carefully. Make your own notes in the margin.

"[1] This would be perfectly obvious—if I weren't a man accustomed to sleeping at night whose experiences while asleep are at least as far-fetched as those that madmen have while awake. How often, at night, I've been convinced that I was here, sitting before the fire, wearing my dressing gown, when in fact I was undressed and between the covers of my bed! [2] But now I am looking at this piece of paper with my eyes wide open; the head that I am shaking has not been lulled to sleep; I put my hand out consciously and deliberately and feel. None of this would be as distinct if I were asleep. [3] As if I can't remember having been tricked by similar thoughts while asleep! When I think very carefully about this, I see so plainly that there are no reliable signs by which I can distinguish sleeping from waking that I am stupefied—and my stupor itself suggests that I am asleep!"

This is an excellent example of the way Descartes proceeds. Remember, I said earlier that sometimes he says things he later decides are false. He says something in 1 that he criticizes in 2, and then in 3 he criticizes what he said in 2 and goes back to 1. It may be more complicated to explain than to read. Reread the section and look for the pattern of statement, criticism, and criticism of criticism.

What he is saying in 1 is _____

_____ . He changes

his mind in 2 by saying, in essence, _____

_____ . However, in 3 he

says _____ .

The main conclusion of the whole passage is _____

_____ .

A few moments ago, you mentioned some occasions when your senses deceived you, but you agreed with Descartes that it would be insane to think they deceived you about very obvious facts, such as the particular location of your body. Then you carefully read his account of dreaming. You certainly could dream that you were reading this book. Perhaps it would be a bad dream! Nonetheless, your senses would tell you that you were slaving away over Descartes when, in fact, your body was in bed. And doesn't something like this happen every night? You are convinced you are one place, running through the woods away from a hairy monster, for example, when in fact you are under the covers in your bedroom.

Have you ever had a very strange dream that you were totally convinced was true?

I dreamed that _____

_____ . Is

Descartes trying to say _____

_____ ?

My answer is that he is saying your senses deceive you every night. Therefore, you can never be 100 percent certain that you are looking at your real body and not your dream body. All you have to do to prove Descartes wrong is give one example of something you can do while awake that you couldn't dream. Then, whenever you need to know if your senses are lying to you, you could try to do this one thing as a test. If you couldn't do it, you would know you were dreaming. If you could do it, you would know you were awake.

One thing I could do to prove I am not dreaming right now

would be to _____ . But, if I am

trying to learn how to think philosophically from Descartes, I

should criticize this by saying _____

_____ .

Another thing I could do right now that I might not be able to do if

I were dreaming would be _____

_____ . But

a strong criticism I could offer against this would be _____

_____ .

I conclude that _____

_____ .

The best minds criticize their own conclusions even better than their critics could. Descartes goes on to give some examples of things that he could be certain of, whether or not he is dreaming.

One page _____ , he mentions _____

_____ .

But then he wonders if perhaps even when he adds the numbers 2 and 3 together he is mistaken. Admittedly, the odds would be very slim. But one can make equally simple mistakes on tests in any math class. Descartes is wondering whether he can ever be totally positive of anything. He is seeking some truth that it would be absolutely inconceivable on any possible occasion to doubt.

Can't I be 100 percent certain that _____ ?

Or would Descartes argue against this by saying _____

_____ ? But

perhaps a better example of a truth that I could be totally positive

of would be the truth that _____

_____ . But

could I offer a strong argument against even this truth by saying

_____ ?

Descartes concludes _Meditation I_ by imagining there is an all-powerful evil demon who is fooling him all the time. He then says, "I will say that sky, air, earth, color, shape, sound, and other external things are just dreamed illusions that the demon uses to ensnare my judgment." In other words?

In other words, _____

_____ .

One reason he imagines this being is to see if there is anything even an all-powerful demon could not deceive him about. Put yourself in his situation.

Very well. I will imagine there is some all-powerful force that has

nothing to do except deceive me. I'll call him Mr. _____ . He has deceived me about who my parents are, about where I was born, and even about the color of my hair and eyes, what I look like, everything. He has found ways to poison my mind and every belief I have, so that I am wrong about everything and know nothing. The

question is whether there is anything even Mr. _____ could not deceive me about. Is there one truth that no force on earth could deceive me about? If there is one such truth, then that would be like the single perfect truth that Descartes is looking for. I am going to say the single truth that not even the all-

powerful and wicked Mr. _____ could deceive me about would

be the truth that _____

_____ .

Would Descartes agree?

Exercise 1.1

Label each of the following statements consistent (C) or inconsistent (I) with the ideas Descartes presents in the first two paragraphs of *Meditation I*.

1. He must show each of his beliefs to be false.

2. It is not possible to achieve certainty about anything.

3. His beliefs have a doubtful, shaky foundation.

4. He should treat beliefs that are slightly doubtful the same as beliefs that are completely doubtful.

5. He will begin by attacking his "foundational" beliefs.

6. All knowledge appears to come through the senses.

Exercise 1.2

Number the following ideas in the order in which Descartes introduces them in *Meditation I*.

a. He might be like a madman.

b. He needs to attack the foundations of his beliefs.

c. He imagines he is dreaming.

d. He asserts that all he has learned has come from his senses.

e. He imagines an evil demon who is fooling him all the time.

f. He does not believe he can tell dreaming from waking.

g. He remembers that his senses occasionally deceive him about objects they cannot perceive clearly.

h. He believes God might be deceiving him about even obvious concepts, such as simple mathematical truths.

i. Whether he is asleep or awake, he can know simple mathematical truths.

j. His dreams must be copies of something real.

Exercise 1.3

In *Meditation I*, Descartes goes back and forth between doubt and certainty. He is fighting an inner war that doubt eventually wins. To see the pattern of the conflict, reread *Meditation I* beginning at paragraph 3. Label every argument that supports certainty *Pro* and every argument that supports doubt *Con*. For example, here is the first paragraph you will read:

"*[Pro]* Of course, whatever I have so far accepted as supremely true I have learned either from the senses or through the senses. *[Con]* But I have occasionally caught the senses deceiving me, and it's prudent never completely to trust those who have cheated us even once."

There are, depending on how you count, approximately six arguments on each side.

MEDITATION II

On the Nature of the Human Mind, Which Is Better Known Than the Body

PREVIEW

Descartes discovers his first 100 percent certitude: "I must finally conclude that the statement 'I am, I exist' must be true whenever I state it or mentally consider it." Next, he carefully expands this truth into the definition of himself as a "thinking thing." Finally, Descartes examines a piece of wax to convince himself that he can know the existence of his mind far more clearly than he can know anything through his senses.

Remember that Descartes is arguing with himself. He is seeking new certitudes by carefully exploring arguments against those certitudes. Pay careful attention to any question Descartes asks himself. Does Descartes' answer to his question increase or decrease his confidence in his knowledge? Label answers *Pro* that increase Descartes' confidence in his knowledge; label answers *Con* that decrease his confidence in his knowledge.

MEDITATION II

Yesterday's meditation has hurled me into doubts so great that I can neither ignore them nor think my way out of them. I am in turmoil, as if I have accidentally fallen into a whirlpool and can neither touch bottom nor swim to the safety of the surface. I will struggle, however, and try to follow the path that I started on yesterday. I will reject whatever is open to the slightest doubt just as though I have found it to be entirely false, and I will continue until I find something certain—or at least until I know for certain that nothing is certain. Archimedes required only one fixed and immovable point to move the whole earth from its place, and I too can hope for great things if I can find even one small thing that is certain and unshakable.

I will suppose, then, that everything I see is unreal. I will believe that my memory is unreliable and that none of what it presents to me ever happened. I have no senses. Body, shape, extension, motion, and place are fantasies. What then is true? Perhaps just that nothing is certain.

But how do I know that there isn't something different from the things just listed that I do not have the slightest reason to doubt? Isn't there a God, or something like one, who puts my thoughts into me? But why should I say so when I may be the author of those thoughts? Well, isn't it at least the case

The major causes of doubt from "yesterday's meditation" are

_____

_____

_____

_____

_____ .

Number each of the places in this paragraph where Descartes seems to change his mind.

29

Underline Descartes' first certitude.

The word "but" introduces important shifts in Descartes' argument. Circle each one on this and the following pages. Paraphrase the idea he is introducing in the margin.

In this paragraph, underline each of the beliefs Descartes was certain about before *Meditation I.*

that I am something? But I now am denying that I have senses and a body. But I stop here. For what follows from these denials? Am I so bound to my body and to my senses that I cannot exist without them? I have convinced myself that there is nothing in the world—no sky, no earth, no minds, no bodies. Doesn't it follow that I don't exist? No, surely I must exist if it's me who is convinced of something. But there is a deceiver, supremely powerful and cunning, whose aim is to see that I am always deceived. But surely I exist, if I am deceived. Let him deceive me all he can, he will never make it the case that I am nothing while I think that I am something. Thus having fully weighed every consideration, I must finally conclude that the statement "I am, I exist" must be true whenever I state it or mentally consider it.

But I do not yet fully understand what this "I" is that must exist. I must guard against inadvertently taking myself to be something other than I am, thereby going wrong even in the knowledge that I put forward as supremely certain and evident. Hence, I will think once again about what I believed myself to be before beginning these meditations. From this conception, I will subtract everything challenged by the reasons for doubt that I produced earlier, until nothing remains except what is certain and indubitable.

What, then, did I formerly take myself to be? A man, of course. But what is a man? Should I say a rational animal? No, because then I would need to ask what an animal is and what it is to be rational. Thus, starting from a single question, I would sink into many that are more difficult, and I do not have the time to waste on such subtleties. Instead, I will look here at the thoughts that occurred to me spontaneously and naturally when I reflected on what I was. The first thought to occur to me was that I have a face, hands, arms, and all the other equipment (also found in corpses) which I call a body. The next thought to occur to me was that I take nourishment, move myself around, sense, and think—that I do things which I trace back to my soul. Either I didn't stop to think about what this soul was, or I imagined it to be a rarified air, or fire, or ether permeating the denser parts of my body. But, about physical objects, I didn't have any doubts whatever: I thought that I distinctly knew their nature. If I had tried to describe my conception of this nature, I might have said this: "When I call something a physical object, I mean that it is capable of being bounded by a shape and limited to a place; that it can fill a space as to exclude other objects from it; that it can be perceived by touch, sight, hearing, taste, and smell; that it can be moved in various ways, not by itself, but by something else in contact with it." I judged that the powers of self-movement, of sensing, and of thinking did not belong to the nature of physical objects, and, in fact, I marveled that there were some physical objects in which these powers could be found.

But what should I think now, while supposing that a supremely powerful and "evil" deceiver completely devotes himself to deceiving me? Can I say that I have any of the things that I have attributed to the nature of physical objects? I concentrate, think, reconsider—but nothing comes to me; I grow tired of the pointless repetition. But what about the things that I have assigned to soul? Nutrition and self-movement? Since I have no body, these are merely illusions. Sensing? But I cannot sense without a body, and in sleep I've seemed to sense many things that I later realized I had not really sensed. Thinking? It comes down to this: Thought and thought alone cannot be taken away from me. I am, I exist. That much is certain. But for how long?

As long as I think—for it may be that, if I completely stopped thinking, I would completely cease to exist. I am not now admitting anything unless it must be true, and I am therefore not admitting that I am anything at all other than a thinking thing—that is, a mind, soul, understanding, or reason (terms whose meaning I did not previously know). I know that I am a real, existing thing, but what kind of thing? As I have said, a thing that thinks.

What else? I will draw up mental images. I'm not the collection of organs called a human body. Nor am I some rarified gas permeating these organs, or air, or fire, or vapor, or breath—for I have supposed that none of these things exist. Still, I am something. But couldn't it be that these things, which I do not yet know about and which I am therefore supposing to be nonexistent, really aren't distinct from the "I" that I know to exist? I don't know, and I'm not going to argue about it now. I can only form judgments on what I do know. I know that I exist, and I ask what the "I" is that I know to exist. It's obvious that this conception of myself doesn't depend on anything that I do not yet know to exist and, therefore, that it does not depend on anything of which I can draw up a mental image. And the words "draw up" point to my mistake. I would truly be creative if I were to have a mental image of what I am, since to have a mental image is just to contemplate the shape or image of a physical object. I now know with certainty that I exist and at the same time that all images—and, more generally, all things associated with the nature of physical objects—may just be dreams. When I keep this in mind, it seems just as absurd to say "I use mental images to help me understand what I am" as it would to say "Now, while awake, I see something true—but, since I don't yet see it clearly enough, I'll go to sleep and let my dreams present it to me more clearly and truly." Thus I know that none of the things that I can comprehend with the aid of mental images bear on my knowledge of myself. And I must carefully draw my mind away from such things if it is to see its own nature distinctly.

But what then am I? A thinking thing. And what is that? Something that doubts, understands, affirms, denies, wills, refuses, and also senses and has mental images.

That's quite a lot, if I really do all of these things. But don't I? Isn't it me who now doubts nearly everything, understands one thing, affirms this thing, refuses to affirm other things, wants to know much more, refuses to be deceived, has mental images (sometimes involuntarily), and is aware of many things "through his senses"? Even if I am always dreaming, and even if my creator does what he can to deceive me, isn't it just as true that I do all these things as that I exist? Are any of these things distinct from my thought? Can any be said to be separate from me? That it's me who doubts, understands, and wills is so obvious that I don't see how it could be more evident. And it's also me who has mental images. While it may be, as I am supposing, that absolutely nothing of which I have a mental image really exists, the ability to have mental images really does exist and is a part of my thought. Finally, it's me who senses—or who seems to gain awareness of physical objects through the senses. For example, I am now seeing light, hearing a noise, and feeling heat. These things are unreal, since I am dreaming. But it is still certain that I seem to see, to hear, and to feel. This seeming cannot be unreal, and it is what is properly called sensing. Strictly speaking, sensing is just thinking.

The single truth Descartes has established thus far is _____

_____

_____ .

He knows this for certain because

_____

_____ .

The reasons for his conclusion in the last two sentences in this paragraph

are _____

_____

_____

_____ .

What he is adding to his definition of himself as a "thinking thing" is

_____

_____

_____

_____ .

The previous topic Descartes now

returns to is his doubt about _____

_____ .

Descartes is now going to convince himself again that he cannot be certain of even the most obvious facts that come through his senses. Underline the important points he makes in this and the next two paragraphs. Add your own explanatory notes in the margin.

From this, I begin to learn a little about what I am. But I still can't stop thinking that I apprehend physical objects, which I picture in mental images and examine with my senses, much more distinctly than I know this unfamiliar "I," of which I cannot form a mental image. I think this, even though it would be astounding if I comprehended things which I've found to be doubtful, unknown, and alien to me more distinctly than the one which I know to be real: my self. But I see what's happening. My mind enjoys wandering, and it won't confine itself to the truth. I will therefore loosen the reigns on my mind for now so that later, when the time is right, I will be able to control it more easily.

Let's consider the things commonly taken to be the most distinctly comprehended: physical objects that we see and touch. Let's not consider physical objects in general, since general conceptions are very often confused. Rather, let's consider one, particular object. Take, for example, this piece of wax. It has just been taken from the honeycomb; it hasn't yet completely lost the taste of honey; it still smells of the flowers from which it was gathered; its color, shape, and size are obvious; it is hard, cold, and easy to touch; it makes a sound when rapped. In short, everything seems to be present in the wax that is required for me to know it as distinctly as possible. But, as I speak, I move the wax toward the fire; it loses what was left of its taste; it gives up its smell; it changes color; it loses its shape; it gets bigger; it melts; it heats up; it becomes difficult to touch; it no longer makes a sound when struck. Is it still the same piece of wax? We must say that it is: no one denies it or thinks otherwise. Then what was there in the wax that I comprehended so distinctly? Certainly nothing that I reached with my senses—for, while everything having to do with taste, smell, sight, touch, and hearing has changed, the same piece of wax remains.

Perhaps what I distinctly knew was neither the sweetness of honey, nor the fragrance of flowers, nor a sound, but a physical object that once appeared to me one way and now appears differently. But what exactly is it of which I now have a mental image? Let's pay careful attention, remove everything that doesn't belong to the wax, and see what's left. Nothing is left except an extended, flexible, and changeable thing. But what is it for this thing to be flexible and changeable? Is it just that the wax can go from round to square and then to triangular, as I have mentally pictured? Of course not. Since I understand that the wax's shape can change in innumerable ways, and since I can't run through all the changes in my imagination, my comprehension of the wax's flexibility and changeability cannot have been produced by my ability to have mental images. And what about the thing that is extended? Are we also ignorant of its extension? Since the extension of the wax increases when the wax melts, increases again when the wax boils, and increases still more when the wax gets hotter, I will be mistaken about what the wax is unless I believe that it can undergo more changes in extension than I can ever encompass with mental images. I must therefore admit that I do not have an image of what the wax is—that I grasp what it is with only my mind. (While I am saying this about a particular piece of wax, it is even more clearly true about wax in general.) What then is this piece of wax that I grasp only with my mind? It is something that I see, feel, and mentally picture—exactly what I believed it to be at the outset. But it must be noted that, despite the appearances, my grasp of the wax is not visual, tactile, or pictorial. Rather, my grasp of the wax is the result of a purely mental inspection, which can be imperfect and confused, as it was once, or clear and distinct, as it is now, depending on how much attention I pay to the things of which the wax consists.

I'm surprised by how prone my mind is to error. Even when I think to myself non-verbally, language stands in my way, and common usage comes close to deceiving me. For, when the wax is present, we say that we see the wax itself, not that we infer its presence from its color and shape. I'm inclined to leap from this fact about language to the conclusion that I learn about the wax by eyesight rather than by purely mental inspection. But, if I happen to look out my window and see men walking in the street, I naturally say that I see the men just as I say that I see the wax. What do I really see, however, but hats and coats that could be covering robots? I *judge* that there are men. Thus I comprehend with my judgment, which is in my mind, objects that I once believed myself to see with my eyes.

One who aspires to wisdom above that of the common man disgraces himself by deriving doubt from common ways of speaking. Let's go on, then, to ask when I most clearly and perfectly grasped what the wax is. Was it when I first looked at the wax and believed my knowledge of it to come from the external senses—or at any rate from the so-called "common sense," the power of having mental images? Or is it now, after I have carefully studied what the wax is and how I come to know it? Doubt would be silly here. For what was distinct in my original conception of the wax? How did that conception differ from that had by animals? When I distinguish the wax from its external forms—when I "undress" it and view it "naked"—there may still be errors in my judgments about it, but I couldn't possibly grasp the wax in this way without a human mind.

What should I say about this mind—or, in other words, about myself? (I am not now admitting that there is anything to me but a mind.) What is this "I" that seems to grasp the wax so distinctly? Don't I know myself much more truly and certainly, and also much more distinctly and plainly, than I know the wax? For, if I base my judgment that the wax exists on the fact that I see it, my seeing it much more obviously implies that I exist. It's possible that what I see is not really wax, and it's even possible that I don't have eyes with which to see—but it clearly is not possible that, when I see (or, what now amounts to the same thing, when I think I see), the "I" that thinks is not a real thing. Similarly, if I base my judgment that the wax exists on the fact that I feel it, the same fact makes it obvious that I exist. If I base my judgment that the wax exists on the fact that I have a mental image of it or on some other fact of this sort, the same thing can obviously be said. And what I've said about the wax applies to everything else that is outside me. Moreover, if I seem to grasp the wax more distinctly when I detect it with several senses than when I detect it with just sight or touch, I must know myself even more distinctly—for every consideration that contributes to my grasp of the piece of wax or to my grasp of any other physical object serves better to reveal the nature of my mind. Besides, the mind has so much in it by which it can make its conception of itself distinct that what comes to it from physical objects hardly seems to matter.

And now I have brought myself back to where I wanted to be. I now know that physical objects are grasped, not by the senses or the power

The reason his grasp of the wax "is not visual, tactile, or pictorial" is

_____

_____

_____

_____

_____

_____ .

What Descartes learned about his senses by examining the wax was

_____

_____

_____ .

What he learned about his mind was

_____

_____

_____ .

Descartes' main point in this

paragraph is _____

_____

_____

_____

_____

_____ .

of having mental images, but by understanding alone. And, since I grasp physical objects in virtue of their being understandable rather than in virtue of their being tangible or visible, I know that I can't grasp anything more easily or plainly than my mind. But, since it takes time to break old habits of thought, I should pause here to allow the length of my contemplation to impress the new thoughts more deeply into my memory.

THINKING ABOUT MEDITATION II

We'll start each of these sessions in the same way. Tell me in a general way what *Meditation II* was about.

The main points Descartes made were _____

_____

_____

_____ .

How would you state the first truth Descartes discovers that not even an all-powerful demon could deceive him about?

On page _____ , he says, " _____

_____ ." This is his first

certitude because _____

_____ . An all-

powerful demon (or even Mr. _____) could not deceive him about this because as soon as the attempt to deceive him

occurred, Descartes would know for certain that _____

_____

because _____ .

I would say the strengths of what he says are _____

_____ .

The major weaknesses I see are _____

_____ .

In Latin, as you may know, Descartes' first certitude is *cogito, ergo sum.* "I think, therefore I am." Though it is not stated in precisely this form in the *Meditations,* it is in his *Discourse on Method.* Sometimes, the assertion *cogito, ergo sum* is held to be a circular argument and therefore invalid. For example, it is a circular argument if I say you can trust me because Jack says I never lie, and you can trust Jack because I say he never lies. In this kind of argument, A proves B and B proves A; therefore, nothing is proved. Now, think about the statement "I think, therefore I am." Can you see why this might be something like a circular argument?

It might be argued that the A part is _____

_____ and the B part is _____

_____ .

The way A appears to prove B is _____

_____ .

The way B appears to prove A is _____

_____ .

Does this show Descartes is arguing in a circle and therefore he has

not found his 100 percent certitude? I would say _____

_____

_____

_____ .

Now go back to pages 32–33 and read the paragraphs again where he talks about the piece of wax. Try to put yourself in Descartes' place. As you make additional notes in the margin, you will begin to understand that with each rereading, philosophical arguments become slightly clearer.

Very well. Let us say I am holding a piece of wax. I am sitting near a fire in my dressing gown. As I examine the wax visually,

I see _____

_____

_____ . It smells _____ .

It feels _____ .

If I knock it on the arm of my rocking chair, it sounds _____

_____ . Now hold it

close to the fire. Everything changes. It appears _____ .

It smells _____ . It feels _____

_____ . And it sticks to the arm of my rocker!
What can I conclude from all this? I must conclude something about what I know with my senses and something about what I know with my mind. What I have learned about things I know through

my senses is _____

_____ . And what I
have learned about what I know with my mind is _____
_____ . This
relates to the statement *cogito, ergo sum* because _____
_____ .

Now read this last paragraph in *Meditation II.* Underline important sections and make your own notes in the margin.

"[1] And now I have brought myself back to where I wanted to be. I now know that physical objects are grasped, not by the senses or the power of having mental images, but by understanding alone. [2] And since I grasp physical objects in virtue of their being understandable rather than in virtue of their being tangible or visible, I know that I can't grasp anything more easily or plainly than my mind. [3] But since it takes time to break old habits of thought, I should pause here to allow the length of my contemplation to impress the new thoughts more deeply into my memory."

What, in general, is he saying in each numbered section?

I conclude that in section 1, Descartes is saying _____
_____ . In section 2, he is
saying _____
_____ . In section 3, he
reminds himself that _____
_____ .

Now, let's look at this important section in more detail. He has just finished examining the wax. Why, in 1, is it obvious to him "that physical objects are grasped, not by the senses or the power of having mental images, but by understanding alone"?

When I imagined I held the wax, I did not really know what it
was through my senses because _____ .
And I couldn't be said to know it through my imagination because when I try to know wax in imagination what happens
is _____ .
_____ . Therefore, I know the
wax only by my understanding because _____
_____ .

In 2, Descartes says, "I can't grasp anything more easily or plainly than my mind." How does he get to this point from what you just said?

Because I cannot be said to know the wax through my senses or my imagination, but only through my intellect, Descartes' point is

that _____

_____

_____ .

In 3, he refers to "new thoughts" and says he will take a while to get accustomed to them. What are these new thoughts and why does he need to think more about them?

In short, the new thoughts are _____ .

And what is difficult to accept about this is _____

_____ . But does Descartes ever discover any other truths he can be 100 percent certain of besides *cogito, ergo sum*?

Exercise 2.1

Label each of the following statements consistent *(C)* or inconsistent *(I)* with ideas Descartes presents in the first *two* paragraphs of *Meditation II*.

1. There is a way to defeat the evil demon.

2. The doubts from *Meditation I* remain.

3. The only certainty may be that there is no certainty.

4. Concepts that can be partially doubted should be treated differently from concepts that can be entirely doubted.

5. Descartes, unlike Archimedes, will need to find more than one indubitable truth.

Exercise 2.2

Label each of the following statements consistent *(C)* or inconsistent *(I)* with ideas Descartes presents in paragraph 3 of *Meditation II*.

1. If Descartes denies that he has senses and a body, then he can't prove that he exists.

2. Descartes proves that God exists.

3. The deceiver could not deceive Descartes into believing he, Descartes, does not exist.

4. Even if there is no physical world, it does not follow that Descartes' mind does not exist.

5. Descartes proves that he exists.

Exercise 2.3

Number the following ideas in the order in which Descartes introduces them in *Meditation II.*

a. He examines the wax with his senses.

b. He knows for certain that he exists.

c. He notes that his mind, rather than his senses, understands the wax clearly.

d. He assumes that he knows nothing for certain.

e. He realizes that his imagination cannot make an accurate mental picture of all the possible shapes that the wax could take.

f. He is a thinking thing.

Exercise 2.4

One benefit of studying Descartes is learning how to reason more effectively. He often uses examples to make a point. Briefly answer the questions that follow each of Descartes' examples.

1. "Archimedes required only one fixed and immovable point to move the whole earth from its place, and I too can hope for great things if I can find even one small thing that is certain and unshakable."
   a. Archimedes is being compared to?
   b. "One fixed and immovable point" is being compared to?
   c. Moving "the whole earth from its place" is being compared to?
   d. The point of this analogy is?

2. "Let's consider the things commonly taken to be the most distinctly comprehended: physical objects that we see and touch. Let's not consider physical objects in general, since general conceptions are very often confused. Rather, let's consider one particular object. Take, for example, this piece of wax."
   a. "Distinctly comprehended" means?
   b. An example of a "general conception" might be?
   c. The goal in examining the wax is to find out about what?
   d. The wax is an example of what?

3. "But, if I happen to look out my window and see men walking in the street, I naturally say that I see the men just as I say that I see the wax. What do I really see, however, but hats and coats that could be covering robots? I *judge* that there are men. Thus I comprehend with my judgment, which is in my mind, objects that I once believed myself to see with my eyes."
   a. The error Descartes believes he makes when he says he "sees" the men and the wax is?
   b. What is the purpose of mentioning "robots"?
   c. What general point is Descartes making about his senses?

d. What general point is Descartes making about judgment?

e. What causes errors of the type described in this example?

f. What does the last sentence conclude?

g. What evidence is offered for the conclusion in the last sentence?

Exercise 2.5: Review

All arguments can be divided into two parts: evidence and conclusion. For example:

1. All men are mortal.

2. Socrates is a man.

3. Therefore, Socrates is a mortal.

Sentences 1 and 2 are evidence that supports the conclusion in sentence 3.

Think back over *Meditations I* and *II*. What evidence, if any, does Descartes offer for each of the following conclusions? (If you need more help in the analysis of arguments, read Appendix B, "Evidence, Conclusions, and Argument Surgery.")

Meditation I

1. The senses cannot be trusted.

2. He cannot be certain that he is sitting beside the fire in his dressing gown.

3. He is not a madman.

4. His dreams must be copies of something real.

5. He can be certain of simple mathematical truths.

6. He cannot be certain of simple mathematical truths.

7. He cannot be certain that God is not a deceiver.

Meditation II

8. The evil demon cannot deceive him about everything.

9. He exists.

10. He is a thinking thing.

11. He can know his essence as a thinking thing more clearly than he can know a piece of wax.

Exercise 2.6: Review

Now grade Descartes' evidence for 1–11. Use the following scale:

A: An excellent argument, strong, sensible, would certainly convince any thoughtful person.

B: A good argument, certainly more convincing than nonconvincing, but some areas need more development and/or might be open to doubt.

C: A flawed argument, certainly not worthy of a great philosopher. Would need significant improvement to convince a thoughtful person.

D: Any thoughtful person would find it a weak, easy-to-attack argument.

F: A terrible argument that would not convince even someone who desperately wanted to be convinced.

1. Grade each argument.

2. Briefly explain your grade.

3. For each argument you graded "C" or lower, offer evidence that shows why Descartes' argument is weak.

MEDITATION III

On God's Existence

PREVIEW OF THE FIRST HALF
OF MEDITATION III

Descartes summarizes his progress and then discovers a test for further certitudes. Anything he knows as "clearly and distinctly" as he knows the truth that he exists must be 100 percent certain. Descartes realizes that until he proves that God exists and is no deceiver, he cannot add to his store of perfect knowledge. Because Descartes has only established himself as a "thinking thing," he investigates the nature of his thoughts to see if this will help him prove God's existence.

Continue to circle the word "but" when it introduces a shift in the argument; note Descartes' answers to the questions he asks himself.

Meditation III is perhaps the most difficult in this book. We will stop halfway through to think about what you read. It probably would be sensible to set aside an hour or two for the second half of the Meditation. Follow my margin notes carefully and add your own.

MEDITATION III

I will now close my eyes, plug my ears, and withdraw all my senses. I will rid my thoughts of the images of physical objects—or, since that's beyond me, I'll write those images off as empty illusions. Talking with myself and looking more deeply into myself, I'll try gradually to come to know myself better. I am a thinking thing—a thing that doubts, affirms, denies, understands a few things, is ignorant of many things, wills, and refuses. I also sense and have mental images. For, as I've noted, even though the things of which I have sensations or mental images may not exist outside me, I'm certain that the modifications of thought called sensations and mental images exist in me insofar as they are just modifications of thought.

That's a summary of all that I really know—or, at any rate, of all that I've so far noticed that I know. I now will examine more carefully whether there are other things in me that I have not yet discovered. I'm certain that I am a thinking thing. Then don't I know what's needed for me to be certain of other things? In this first knowledge, there is nothing but a clear and distinct grasp of what I affirm, and this grasp surely would not suffice to make me certain if it could ever happen that something I grasped so clearly and distinctly was false. Accordingly, I seem to be able to establish the general rule that whatever I clearly and distinctly grasp is true.

But, in the past, I've accepted as completely obvious and certain many thoughts that I later found to be dubious. What were these thoughts about? The earth, the sky, the stars, and other objects of sense. But what did I clearly grasp about these objects? Only that ideas or thoughts of them

List what you believe you know clearly and distinctly. _____ _____ _____ _____ _____.

List what you know less clearly and less distinctly. _____ _____ _____ _____ _____.

What Descartes knows clearly and distinctly is _____ _____ _____ _____.

41

Assume Descartes is looking up toward the sky. At this point in the argument, he can be certain

that _____

_____

_____ .

But he can have no certainty

that _____

_____

_____ .

Underline the sentence in which he returns to his first certitude.

Eventually, what he must determine

about God is _____

_____

_____

_____ .

because _____

_____

_____ .

Descartes' point in the last sentence

in this paragraph is _____

_____

_____

_____

because _____

_____

_____

_____

_____ .

appeared in my mind. Even now, I don't deny that these ideas occur in me. But there was something else that I used to affirm—something that I used to believe myself to grasp clearly but did not really grasp at all: I affirmed that there were things besides me, that the ideas in me came from these things, and that the ideas perfectly resembled these things. Either I erred here, or I reached a true judgment that wasn't justified by the strength of my understanding.

But what follows? When I considered very simple and easy points of arithmetic or geometry—such as that two and three together make five— didn't I see them clearly enough to affirm their truth? My only reason for judging that I ought to doubt these things was the thought that my God-given nature might deceive me even about what seems most obvious. Whenever I conceive of an all-powerful God, I'm compelled to admit that, if He wants, He can make it the case that I err even about what I take my mind's eye to see most clearly. But, when I turn to the things that I believe myself to grasp very clearly, I'm so convinced by them that I spontaneously burst forth saying, "Whoever may deceive me, he will never bring it about that I am nothing while I think that I am something, or that I have never been when it is now true that I am, or that two plus three is either more or less than five, or that something else in which I recognize an obvious inconsistency is true." And, since I have no reason for thinking that God is a deceiver—indeed, since I don't yet know whether God exists—the grounds for doubt that rest on the supposition that God deceives are very weak and "metaphysical." Still, to rid myself of these grounds, I ought to ask as soon as possible whether there is a God and, if so, whether He can be a deceiver. For it seems that, until I know these two things, I can never be completely certain of anything else.

The structure of my project seems to require, however, that I first categorize my thoughts and ask in which of them truth and falsity really reside. Some of my thoughts are like images of things, and only these can properly be called ideas. I have an idea, for example, when I think of a man, of a chimera, of heaven, of an angel, or of God. But other thoughts have other properties: while I always apprehend something as the object of my thought when I will, fear, affirm, or deny, these thoughts also include a component in addition to the likeness of that thing. Some of these components are called volitions or emotions; others, judgments.

Now, viewed in themselves and without regard to other things, ideas cannot really be false. If I imagine a chimera and a goat, it is just as true that I imagine the chimera as that I imagine the goat. And I needn't worry about falsehood in volitions or emotions. If I have a perverse desire for something, or if I want something that doesn't exist, it's still true that I want that thing. All that remains, then, are my judgments; it's here that I must be careful not to err. And the first and foremost of the errors that I find in my judgments is that of assuming that the ideas in me have a similarity or conformity to things outside me. For, if I were to regard ideas merely as modifications of thought, they could not really provide me with any opportunity for error.

Of my ideas, some seem to me to be innate, others acquired, and others produced by me. The ideas by which I understand reality, truth, and thought seem to have come from my own nature. Those ideas by which I hear a noise, see the sun, or feel the fire I formerly judged to come from things outside me.

And the ideas of sirens, hippogriffs, and so on I have formed in myself. Or maybe I can take all of my ideas to be acquired, all innate, or all created by me: I do not yet clearly see where my ideas come from.

For the moment, the central question is about the ideas that I view as derived from objects existing outside me. What reason is there for thinking that these ideas resemble the objects? I seem to have been taught this by nature. Besides, I find that these ideas are independent of my will and hence of me—for they often appear when I do not want them to do so. For example, I now feel heat whether I want to or not, and I therefore take the idea or sensation of heat to come from something distinct from me: the heat of the fire by which I am not sitting. And the obvious thing to think is that a thing sends me its own likeness, not something else.

I will now see whether these reasons are good enough. When I say that nature teaches me something, I mean just that I have a spontaneous impulse to believe it, not that the light of nature reveals the thing's truth to me. There is an important difference. When the light of nature reveals something to me (such as that my thinking implies my existing) that thing is completely beyond doubt, since there is no faculty as reliable as the light of nature by means of which I could learn that the thing is not true. But, as for my natural impulses, I have often judged them to have led me astray in choices about what's good, and I don't see why I should regard them as any more reliable on matters concerning truth and falsehood.

Next, while my sensory ideas may not depend on my will, it doesn't follow that they come from outside me. While the natural impulses of which I just spoke are in me, they seem to conflict with my will. Similarly, I may have in me an as yet undiscovered ability to produce the ideas that seem to come from outside me—in the way that I used to think that ideas came to me in dreams.

Finally, even if some of my ideas do come from things distinct from me, it doesn't follow that they are likenesses of these things. Indeed, it often seems to me that an idea differs greatly from its cause. For example, I find in myself two different ideas of the sun. One, which I "take in" through the senses and which I ought therefore to view as a typical acquired idea, makes the sun look very small to me. The other, which I derive from astronomical reasoning (that is, which I make, perhaps by composing it from innate ideas), pictures the sun as many times larger than the earth. It clearly cannot be that both of these ideas are accurate likenesses of a sun that exists outside me, and reason convinces me that the one least like the sun is the one that seems to arise most directly from it.

All that I've said shows that, until now, my belief that there are things outside me that send their ideas or images to me (perhaps through my senses) has rested on blind impulse rather than certain judgment.

Still, it seems to me that there may be a way of telling whether my ideas come from things that exist outside me. Insofar as the ideas of things are just modifications of thought, I find no inequality among them; all seem to arise from me in the same way. But, insofar as different ideas present different things to me, there obviously are great differences among them. The ideas of substances are unquestionably greater—or have more "subjective reality"—than those of modifications or accidents. Similarly, the idea by which I understand the supreme God—eternal, infinite, omniscient,

An example of an innate idea might be _____ _____ _____ ;

an example of an acquired idea might be _____ _____ _____ ;

an example of a created idea might be _____ _____ _____ .

"Light of nature" is Descartes' phrase for reason.

One idea Descartes has about the sun is _____ _____ , and the other idea is _____ _____ .

The idea that appears least true about the sun is _____ _____ because _____ _____ _____ .

The main problem Descartes is trying to solve in this Meditation is _____ _____ _____ _____ _____ .

omnipotent, and creator of all things other than Himself—has more subjective reality in it than the ideas of finite substances.

THINKING ABOUT THE FIRST HALF
OF MEDITATION III

Let's halt here for a few moments of reflection. What, in general, has Descartes been thinking about?

The major points I noted were _____

_____

_____

_____ .

How can Descartes tell when he has arrived at his goal of finding 100 percent certitudes? He can he tell the difference between a concept that is 99.99 percent certain and one that is perfectly, 100 percent, certain?

His first 100 percent certitude is, of course, "I think, therefore I exist." He realizes at the beginning of *Meditation III* that he has discovered not only a perfect certitude in this statement but also a way of measuring the certainty of other statements. He grasps the perfect truth of "I think, therefore I exist" with "clarity and distinctness." Any other claim that he grasps in this same way will be equally certain. Thus, we might say that Descartes can tell if he has found other 100 percent certitudes when he grasps them with 100 percent clarity and 100 percent distinctness.

Using your list of truths on page 9 and any other concepts you wish, fill in the following scale by making five statements and labeling each for clarity and distinctness. (Instead of focusing on the truth of the statement, focus on how clearly and distinctly you grasp the truth of the statement.)

100 percent clarity and distinctness: _____

___ percent clarity and distinctness: _____

___ percent clarity and distinctness: _____

___ percent clarity and distinctness: _____

___ percent clarity and distinctness: _____

0 percent clarity and distinctness: _____

Now compare this scale with the statements you made in the "Thinking Like Descartes" section at the beginning of the book. Has reading Descartes produced any differences in the way you think about what you know?

Rereading my responses in "Thinking Like Descartes," I notice

_____

_____ .

Comparing this with the clarity and distinctness scale, I realize

_____

_____ .

Now we are going to reread two sections in which Descartes carefully thinks over the source of mental errors. This is obviously an important topic if he is looking for truths he can be 100 percent certain about. His search will be greatly simplified if he can find some general rules for telling true ideas from false ideas. Add your own underlining to the following. Your margin notes should simply try to put Descartes' ideas into your own language.

"All that remains, then, are my judgments; it's here that I must be careful not to err. And the first and foremost of the errors that I find in my judgments is that of assuming that the ideas in me have a similarity or conformity to things outside me. For, if I were to regard ideas merely as modifications of thought, they could not really provide me with any opportunity for error."

You are standing in the desert. Ahead you see a shimmering lake. You thus have the idea in your mind of a lake. What is true and what is false about this idea?

What is true about the idea in my mind is simply _____

_____ . What would lead me to error would be

to judge that the idea in my mind is _____ . Thus, mental

errors about my senses arise when _____

_____ .

What Descartes means when he says, "If I were to regard ideas merely as modifications of thought they could not really provide

me with any opportunity for error," is _____

_____ . And

how this relates to the idea of the lake in my mind is _____

_____ .

Now read the following section, adding your own underlining and margin notes.

"[1] . . . it often seems to me that an idea differs greatly from its cause. [2] For example, I find in myself two different ideas of the sun. One, which I 'take in' through the senses and which I ought therefore to view as a typical acquired idea, makes the sun look very small to me. The other, which I derive from astronomical reasoning (that is, which I make, perhaps by composing it from innate ideas), pictures the sun as many times larger than the earth. It clearly cannot be that both of these ideas are accurate likenesses of a sun that exists outside me, and reason convinces me that the one least like the sun is the one that seems to arise most directly from it.

[3] All that I've said shows that, until now, my belief that there are things outside me that send their ideas or images to me (perhaps through my senses) has rested on blind impulse rather than certain judgment."

Start with 1. Give me two examples of differences you have experienced between "an idea" and "its cause."

Let us say the idea is _____ and the cause is _____ . The obvious difference is _____ _____ . One of the most common examples of this might be the cause _____ and the mistaken idea of _____ . The difference is _____ .

Fine. Now put yourself in Descartes' place and think about the sun as he does in 2.

Very well. I am looking at the sun. The idea that I have of the sun that comes through my eyes is _____ . But I have another idea of the sun, which is perhaps born with me as he says. This second idea of the sun is _____ . The difference between these two ideas is _____ _____ . Error would arise in the case of the first idea only if I _____ .

Now read 3 again—probably for the third or fourth time! It is central to *Meditation III*.

The essential point he is making in 3 is _____ _____ .

Exercise 3.1

Arrange the following concepts in the order in which Descartes presents them in the first half of *Meditation III*.

a. He has discovered no evidence proving that his sensory ideas are accurate copies of objects.

b. He must prove that God exists and that God is no deceiver before he can discover other certitudes.

c. He categorizes his thoughts into volitions, emotions, and judgments.

d. A clear and distinct grasp of something is required to know a thing for certain.

e. The light of nature is different from natural impulse.

f. His ideas are either innate, acquired, or produced by him.

Exercise 3.2

(If you need help in the analysis of arguments, read Appendix B.)

1. Paraphrase the first argument in paragraph 8 ("For the moment, the central question . . ."). Because _____

   _____ .

   Therefore, _____

   _____ .

2. Paraphrase the first argument in paragraph 9 ("I will now see whether these reasons . . ."). Because _____

   _____ .

   Therefore, _____

   _____ .

3. Paraphrase the first argument in paragraph 10 ("Next, while my sensory ideas may not . . ."). Because _____

   _____ .

   Therefore, _____

   _____ .

4. Paraphrase the first argument in paragraph 11 ("Finally, even if some of my ideas . . ."). Because _____

   _____ .

   Therefore, _____

   _____ .

5. Now look at paragraphs 8, 9, 10, and 11. Paragraph(s) _____

   _____ refute(s) arguments in paragraph(s) _____ .

Exercise 3.3

All arguments can be divided into two parts: evidence and conclusion. The evidence is presented as reason for believing the conclusion. Evidence can be thought of as one or more "because" statements that lead to a "therefore" statement in the conclusion.

(Because) Socrates is a human.
(Because) All humans are mortals.
(Therefore) Socrates is a mortal.

Underline the conclusion, the "therefore" statement, in each of the following arguments.

1. I think I exist. I can be absolutely certain I exist. I must exist in order to think I exist.

2. I cannot tell for certain that external objects exist. I cannot tell if my ideas are accurate copies of external objects. If my ideas are not accurate copies of external objects, then I cannot know for certain that external objects exist.

3. God could be deceiving me. God is all-powerful.

4. It is not possible that anything I've grasped clearly and distinctly could be false. In the future, I can use it as a general rule that anything I grasp clearly and distinctly is true.

5. I need to prove that God is no deceiver. God might be deceiving me. If God is deceiving me, then I can't know anything for certain.

6. I should be careful when I make judgments about my ideas being copies of external objects. I can make errors when I judge that my ideas are copies of external objects.

Exercise 3.4

Omitting argument 1, arrange the arguments in 3.3 in the order in which they occur in *Meditation III,* and give the paragraph number of each argument.

PREVIEW OF THE SECOND HALF OF MEDITATION III

In the concluding section of *Meditation III,* Descartes introduces a number of difficult concepts: subjective reality, formal reality, eminent reality, and reality being "transferred" from cause to effect.

Subjective reality is the reality of ideas. Formal reality is, among other things, the reality of the physical world. Eminent reality, it will turn out, is God's reality. For Descartes, subjective reality is "less real" than formal reality and formal reality is "less real" than eminent reality. This is hard for modern readers to grasp because we usually think of something as either "real" or "not real," without "more" or "less" in between. A lake is real; a mirage is not real. A person is real; a dragon is not real.

To get a sense of Descartes' way of thinking consider three things: the actual Pocahontas, the Disney animated film *Pocahontas,* and a dream about the Disney film. The actual Pocahontas could be said to be more real than the Disney film, and the Disney film could be said to be more real than a dream about the film. If Pocahontas hadn't existed, then the film *Pocahontas* wouldn't exist; if the film *Pocahontas* didn't exist, then the dream about the film wouldn't exist. Similarly for Descartes, God is more real than the physical world and the physical world is more real than ideas about the physical world. If God didn't exist, then the physical world wouldn't exist; if the physical world didn't exist, then ideas about the physical world wouldn't exist. God's eminent reality makes possible the physical world's formal reality, which, in turn, makes possible ideas' subjective reality.

Descartes holds that these realities influence each other in a special, one-directional way. Something "more real" can be the cause of something "less real," but not vice versa. God can be the cause of the reality of a physical object, not vice versa. A physical object can be the cause of an idea of a physical object, but not vice versa. Descartes' way of stating this one-directional influence is to say that the degree of reality in the cause is always equal to or greater than the degree of reality in the effect.

This concept of reality and cause and effect is important for the proof of God's existence that Descartes develops in the following section from *Meditation III*. God, remember, has eminent reality. Descartes' idea of God is therefore an idea of a being with eminent reality. Descartes himself has merely formal reality. Therefore, Descartes could not be the cause of his idea of God. Descartes has too little reality! Only God could be the cause of Descartes' idea of God. Therefore, God exists.

MEDITATION III (continued)

Now, the light of nature reveals that there is at least as much in a complete efficient cause as in its effect. For where could an effect get its reality if not from its cause? And how could a cause give something unless it had it? It follows both that something cannot come from nothing and that what is more perfect—that is, has more reality in it—cannot come from what is less perfect or has less reality. This obviously holds, not just for those effects whose reality is actual or formal, but also for ideas, whose reality we regard as merely subjective. For example, it's impossible for a nonexistent stone to come into existence unless it's produced by something containing, either formally or eminently, everything in the stone. Similarly, heat can only be induced in something that's not already hot by something having at least the same degree of perfection as heat. Also, it's impossible for the *idea* of heat or of stone to be in me unless it's been put there by a cause having at least as much reality as I conceive of in the heat or the stone. For, although the cause doesn't transmit any of its actual or formal reality to the idea, we shouldn't infer that it can be less real than the idea; all that we can infer is that by its nature the idea doesn't require any formal reality except what it derives from my thought, of which it is a modification. Yet, as the idea contains one particular subjective reality rather than another, it must get this reality from a cause having at least as much formal reality as the idea has subjective reality. For, if we suppose that an idea has something in it that wasn't in its cause, we must suppose that it got this thing from nothing. However imperfect the existence of something that exists subjectively in the understanding through an idea, it obviously is something, and it therefore cannot come from nothing.

Underline each important point in this paragraph. Add your own paraphrase in the margin.

An example of a cause would

be _____ ,
and the effect it creates would

be _____

_____ .

Circle each "it" in this paragraph and draw an arrow to the word or phrase referred to.

The last sentence, "Hence, the light . . ." is the conclusion of an argument. Reread this and the preceding paragraph several times. Number each important point that leads to this conclusion. Essentially,

Descartes is arguing _____

_____

_____

_____

because _____

_____

_____

_____

_____ .

Descartes is looking for an idea that could not have originated from himself. Underline this unique idea when you find it.

And, although the reality that I'm considering in my ideas is just subjective, I ought not to suspect that it can fail to be in an idea's cause formally—that it's enough for it to be there subjectively. For, just as the subjective existence of my ideas belongs to the ideas in virtue of their nature, the formal existence of the ideas' causes belongs to those causes—or, at least, to the first and foremost of them—in virtue of the causes' nature. Although one idea may arise from another, this can't go back to infinity; we must eventually arrive at a primary idea whose cause is an "archetype" containing formally all the reality that the idea contains subjectively. Hence, the light of nature makes it clear to me that the ideas in me are like images that may well fall short of the things from which they derive, but cannot contain anything greater or more perfect.

The more time and care I take in studying this, the more clearly and distinctly I know it to be true. But what follows from it? If I can be sure that the subjective reality of one of my ideas is so great that it isn't in me either formally or eminently and hence that I cannot be the cause of that idea, I can infer that I am not alone in the world—that there exists something else that is the cause of the idea. But, if I can find no such idea in me, I will have no argument at all for the existence of anything other than me—for, having diligently searched for such an argument, I have yet to find one.

Of my ideas—besides my idea of myself, about which there can be no problem here—one presents God, others inanimate physical objects, others angels, others animals, and still others men like me.

As to my ideas of other men, of animals, and of angels, it's easy to see that—even if the world contained no men but me, no animals, and no angels—I could have composed these ideas from those that I have of myself, of physical objects, and of God.

And, as to my ideas of physical objects, it seems that nothing in them is so great that it couldn't have come from me. For, if I analyze my ideas of physical objects carefully, taking them one by one as I did yesterday when examining my idea of the piece of wax, I notice that there is very little in them that I grasp clearly and distinctly. What I do grasp clearly and distinctly in these ideas is size (which is extension in length, breadth, and depth), shape (which arises from extension's limits), position (which the differently shaped things have relative to one another), and motion (which is just change of position). To these I can add substance, duration, and number. But my thoughts of other things in physical objects (such as light and color, sound, odor, taste, heat and cold, and tactile qualities) are so confused and obscure that I can't say whether they are true or false—whether my ideas of these things are of something or of nothing. Although, as I noted earlier, that which is properly called falsehood—namely, *formal* falsehood—can only be found in judgments, we can still find falsehood of another sort—namely, *material* falsehood—in an idea when it presents what is not a thing as though it were a thing. For example, the ideas that I have of coldness and heat are so unclear and indistinct that I can't tell from them whether coldness is just the absence of heat, or heat just the absence of coldness, or both are real qualities, or neither is. And, since every idea is "of something," the idea that presents coldness to me as something real and positive could justifiably be called false if coldness were just the absence of heat. And the same holds for other ideas of this sort.

For such ideas, I need not posit a creator distinct from me. I know by the light of nature that, if one of these ideas is false—that is, if it doesn't present a real thing—it comes from nothing—that is, the only cause of its being in me is a deficiency of my nature, which clearly is imperfect. If one of these ideas is true, however, I still see no reason why I couldn't have produced it myself—for these ideas present so little reality to me that I can't even distinguish it from nothing.

Of the things that are clear and distinct in my ideas of physical objects, it seems that I may have borrowed some—such as substance, duration, and number—from my idea of myself. I think of the stone as a substance—that is, as something that can exist on its own—just as I think of myself as a substance. Although I conceive of myself as a thinking and unextended thing and of the stone as an extended and unthinking thing so that the two conceptions are quite different, they are the same in that they both seem to be of substances. And, when I grasp that I exist now while remembering that I existed in the past, or when I count my various thoughts, I get the idea of duration or number, which I can then apply to other things. The other components of my ideas of physical objects—extension, shape, place, and motion—can't be in me formally, since I'm just a thinking thing. But, as these things are just modes of substance, and as I am a substance, it seems that they may be in me eminently.

All that's left is my idea of God. Is there something in this idea of God that couldn't have come from me? By "God" I mean a substance that's infinite, independent, supremely intelligent, and supremely powerful—the thing from which I and everything else that may exist derive our existence. The more I consider these attributes, the less it seems that they could have come from me alone. So I must conclude that God necessarily exists.

While I may have the idea of substance in me by virtue of my being a substance, I who am finite would not have the idea of infinite substance in me unless it came from a substance that really was infinite.

And I shouldn't think that, rather than having a true idea of infinity, I grasp it merely as the absence of limits—in the way that I grasp rest as the absence of motion and darkness as the absence of light. On the contrary, it's clear to me that there is more reality in an infinite than in a finite substance and hence that my grasp of the infinite must somehow be prior to my grasp of the finite—my understanding of God prior to my understanding of myself. For how could I understand that I doubt and desire, that I am deficient and imperfect, if I didn't have the idea of something more perfect to use as a standard of comparison?

And, unlike the ideas of hot and cold which I just discussed, the idea of God cannot be said to be materially false and hence to come from nothing. On the contrary, since the idea of God is completely clear and distinct and contains more subjective reality than any other idea, no idea is truer *per se* and none less open to the suspicion of falsity. The idea of a supremely perfect and infinite entity is, I maintain, completely true. For, while I may be able to suppose that there is no such entity, I can't even suppose (as I did about the idea of coldness) that my idea of God fails to show me something real. This idea is maximally clear and distinct, for it contains everything that I grasp clearly and distinctly, everything real and true, everything with any perfection. It doesn't matter that I can't fully comprehend the infinite—that

"Such ideas" refers back to _____
_____
_____ .

The possible origin of his idea of

"duration or number" is _____

_____

_____ .

He concludes that God exists

because _____

_____

_____

_____

_____ .

Look again at Ronald Rubin's preface (pp. vii–ix) for a distinction between subjective, formal, and eminent reality.

The idea of God is "most true"

because _____

_____

_____

_____

_____

_____ .

The doubt he raises concerning his

previous view of God is _____

_____

_____

_____ .

Underline the sentences in which he
refutes the doubt in the previous
paragraph.

The new question he raises now is

_____

_____ .

The reason he raises the new

question is _____

_____

_____ .

The four possible sources for his
existence are

1. _____

2. _____

3. _____

4. _____

The source he investigates first is

_____ .

there are innumerable things in God which I can't comprehend fully or even
reach with thought. Because of the nature of the infinite, I who am finite
cannot comprehend it. It's enough that I think about the infinite and judge
that, if I grasp something clearly and distinctly and know it to have some
perfection, it's present either formally or eminently—perhaps along with
innumerable other things of which I am ignorant—in God. If I do this, then
of all my ideas the idea of God will be most true and most clear and distinct.

But maybe I am greater than I have assumed; maybe all the perfections
that I attribute to God are in me potentially, still unreal and unactualized. I
have already seen my knowledge gradually increase, and I don't see anything to prevent its becoming greater and greater to infinity. Nor do I see
why, by means of such increased knowledge, I couldn't get all the rest of
God's perfections. Finally, if the potential for these perfections is in me, I
don't see why that potential couldn't account for the production of the
ideas of these perfections in me.

None of this is possible. First, while it's true that my knowledge gradually increases and that I have many as yet unactualized potentialities, none
of this fits with my idea of God, in whom absolutely nothing is potential;
indeed, the gradual increase in my knowledge shows that I am *imperfect*.
Besides, I see that, even if my knowledge were continually to become
greater and greater, it would never become actually infinite, since it would
never become so great as to be unable to increase. But I judge God to be
actually infinite so that nothing can be added to his perfection. Finally, I see
that an idea's subjective being must be produced, not by mere potentiality
(which, strictly speaking, is nothing), but by what is actual or formal.

When I pay attention to these things, the light of nature makes all of
them obvious. But, when I attend less carefully and the images of sensible
things blind my mind's eye, it's not easy for me to remember why the idea
of an entity more perfect than I am must come from an entity that really is
more perfect. That's why I'll go on to ask whether I, who have the idea of a
perfect entity, could exist if no such entity existed.

From what might I derive my existence if not from God? Either from
myself, or from my parents, or from something else less perfect than God—
for nothing more perfect than God, or even as perfect as Him, can be
thought of or imagined.

But, if I derived my existence from myself, I wouldn't doubt, or want,
or lack anything. I would have given myself every perfection of which I
have an idea, and thus I myself would be God. And I shouldn't think that
it might be harder to give myself what I lack than what I already have. On
the contrary, it would obviously be much harder for me, a thinking thing
or substance, to emerge from nothing than for me to give myself knowledge of the many things of which I am ignorant, which is just an attribute
of substance. But surely, if I had given myself that which is harder to get, I
wouldn't have denied myself complete knowledge, which would have
been easier to get. Indeed, I wouldn't have denied myself *any* of the perfections that I grasp in the idea of God. None of these perfections seems
harder to get than existence. But, if I had given myself everything that I
now have, these perfections would have seemed harder to get than existence if they were harder to get—for in creating myself I would have discovered the limits of my power.

I can't avoid the force of this argument by supposing that, since I've always existed as I do now, there's no point in looking for my creator. Since my lifetime can be divided into innumerable parts each of which is independent of the others, the fact that I existed a little while ago does not entail that I exist now, unless a cause "re-creates" me—or, in other words, preserves me—at this moment. For, when we attend to the nature of time, it's obvious that exactly the same power and action are required to preserve a thing at each moment through which it endures as would be required to create it anew if it had never existed. Hence, one of the things revealed by the light of nature is that preservation and creation differ only in the way we think of them.

I ought to ask myself, then, whether I have the power to ensure that I, who now am, will exist in a little while. Since I am nothing but a thinking thing—or, at any rate, since I am now focusing on the part of me that thinks—I would surely be aware of this power if it were in me. But I find no such power. And from this I clearly see that there is an entity distinct from me on whom I depend.

> "This power" refers to _____
> _____ .

But maybe this entity isn't God. Maybe I am the product of my parents or of some other cause less perfect than God. No. As I've said, there must be at least as much in a cause as in its effect. Hence, since I am a thinking thing with the idea of God in me, my cause, whatever it may be, must be a thinking thing having in it the idea of every perfection that I attribute to God. And we can go on to ask whether this thing gets its existence from itself or from something else. If it gets its existence from itself, it's obvious from what I've said that it must be God—for it would have the power to exist on its own and hence the power actually to give itself every perfection of which it has an idea, including every perfection that I conceive of in God. But, if my cause gets its existence from some other thing, we can go on to ask whether this other thing gets its existence from itself or from something else. Eventually, we will come to the ultimate cause, which will be God.

It's clear enough that there can't be an infinite regress here—especially since I am concerned, not so much with the cause that originally produced me, as with the one that preserves me at the present moment.

And I can't suppose that several partial causes combined to make me or that I get the ideas of the various perfections that I attribute to God from different causes so that, while each of these perfections can be found somewhere in the universe, there is no God in whom they all come together. On the contrary, one of the chief perfections that I understand God to have is unity, simplicity, inseparability from everything in Him. Surely the idea of the unity of all God's perfections can only have been put in me by a cause that gives me the ideas of all the other perfections—for nothing could make me aware of the unbreakable connection of God's perfections unless it made me aware of what those perfections are.

> His problem in the first sentence is
> _____
> _____
> _____ .
> His answer is _____
> _____
> _____ .

Finally, even if everything that I used to believe about my parents is true, it's clear that they don't preserve me. Insofar as I am a thinking thing, they did not even take part in creating me. They simply formed the matter in which I used to think that I (that is, my mind, which is all I am now taking myself to be) resided. There can therefore be no problem about my parents. And I am driven to this conclusion: The fact that I exist and have an idea in me of a perfect entity—that is, God—conclusively entails that God does in fact exist.

> Underline the source of his idea of God.

The source of his idea of God cannot

be _____

because _____

_____

_____ .

Nor can the source be _____

_____

_____

because _____

_____

_____ .

The source of his idea of God must

be _____

_____

because _____

_____

_____

_____ .

The reason God cannot be a deceiver

is_____

_____

_____

_____ .

Descartes achieves a pinnacle in the

last paragraph. It is _____

_____

_____ .

All that's left is to explain how I have gotten my idea of God from Him. I have not taken it in through my senses; it has never come to me unexpectedly as the ideas of sensible things do when those things affect (or seem to affect) my external organs of sense. Nor have I made the idea myself; I can't subtract from it or add to it. The only other possibility is that the idea is innate in me, like my idea of myself.

It's not at all surprising that in creating me God put this idea into me, impressing it on His work like a craftsman's mark (which needn't be distinct from the work itself). The very fact that it was God who created me confirms that I have somehow been made in His image or likeness and that I grasp this likeness, which contains the idea of God, in the same way that I grasp myself. Thus, when I turn my mind's eye on myself, I understand, not just that I am an incomplete and dependent thing which constantly strives for bigger and better things, but also that He on whom I depend has all these things in Himself as infinite reality rather than just as vague potentiality and hence that He must be God. The whole argument comes down to this: I know that I could not exist with my present nature—that is, that I could not exist with the idea of God in me—unless there really were a God. This must be the very God whose idea is in me, the thing having all of the perfections that I can't fully comprehend but can somehow reach with thought, who clearly cannot have any defects. From this, it's obvious that He can't deceive—for, as the natural light reveals, fraud and deception arise from defect.

But before examining this more carefully and investigating its consequences, I want to dwell for a moment in the contemplation of God, to ponder His attributes, to see and admire and adore the beauty of His boundless light, insofar as my clouded insight allows. As I have faith that the supreme happiness of the next life consists wholly of the contemplation of divine greatness, I now find that contemplation of the same sort, though less perfect, affords the greatest joy available in this life.

THINKING ABOUT MEDITATION III

Begin as before by thinking back over what you read and summarizing your general impression.

The points that Descartes made that I understand most clearly were

_____

_____

_____ .

In the second half of *Meditation III,* which you just read, Descartes presents two proofs for God's existence. I will guide you through the first proof and summarize the second.

In the first proof, Descartes begins by looking for some idea in his mind that he could not have caused. In other words, if he can find some idea that did not come from him, the idea must have come from somewhere else. Thus, he can add to the 100 percent certitudes he is seeking that something exists outside himself (and this something else will turn out to be God). Remember that until halfway through *Meditation III*, he has only proved his own existence, defined himself as a thinking thing, and established some general rules for telling true ideas from false ideas. In the section below, which you have already read once, he sets up a general rule for telling if one of his ideas must have originated from something other than himself.

"If I can be sure that the subjective reality of one of my ideas is so great that it isn't in me either formally or eminently and hence that I cannot be the cause of that idea, I can infer that I am not alone in the world—that there exists something else that is the cause of the idea. But, if I can find no such idea in me, I will have no argument at all for the existence of anything other than me. . . ."

As he sorts through the ideas in his mind, what is he looking for?

Looking carefully at the first sentence in the quotation, I would say

he is looking for _____ .

If he finds this, he will know _____ .

If he doesn't find this, he will have to conclude _____

_____ . Therefore, it is important that he find what he is looking for!

Sometimes very simple examples help. I'll offer one and you can add your own. My uncle dug a fishpond. He stocked the pond with perch. One day, he caught a large fish that he couldn't identify. If the fish was a perch, then he could conclude that it probably had been produced by the fish in the pond. If the fish wasn't a perch, he could conclude that some outside source (a friendly neighbor?) had put it there. Descartes is looking through the ideas in his head. If he finds one that could not have come from other ideas in his head or that could not have come from him, then he can conclude that it came from somewhere else. And, it seems, he can know this with 100 percent certitude. Now try your example.

My example is _____

_____ . This is like Descartes' situation

because _____

_____ .

And what is this idea that he believes he could not be the cause of?

I don't think I would be wrong if I said the idea is _____

_____ .

Something tells me that if you are not right, you soon will be. Read this, another passage from *Meditation III*.

"All that's left is my idea of God. Is there anything in this idea of God that couldn't have come from me? By 'God' I mean a substance that's infinite, independent, supremely intelligent, and supremely powerful—the thing from which I and everything else that may exist derive our existence. The more I consider these attributes, the less it seems that they could have come from me alone. So I must conclude that God necessarily exists.

"While I may have the idea of substance in me by virtue of my being a substance, I who am finite would not have the idea of infinite substance in me unless it came from a substance that really was infinite."

Try to think through this as Descartes would.

An interesting problem. I have looked through all the ideas in my mind, searching to see if there are any that could not have come

from my own mind. At last, I come to the idea of _____ .
As I examine this idea, I define it as the idea of a being who is

_____ .

Now, why couldn't this idea have come from my own mind? The answer must lie in a description of what I know myself to be and what is peculiarly different about this idea. I am a being who is

_____ . This idea is about a

being who is _____ .

Therefore, this idea could not have come from me because _____

_____ .

Through much of *Meditation III*, Descartes discusses cause and effect and relates these concepts to both his first and his second proof of God's existence. Try to do the same.

An example of a cause is _____ . The effect it produces is

_____ . The question is, applying this to Descartes' first proof of God's existence, is the idea of God in my mind the cause or the effect? And, whichever it is, how does this relate to the argument that God, not I, produced the idea? I will say that when I think

of God and the idea of God in my mind, the cause is _____

and the effect is _____ and this can be used to show that God

exists because _____ .

Thus, I could not be the cause of the idea because _____ .

Now let's move on to Descartes' second proof of God's existence. Here is a key section from that proof. Underline important parts and put your own examples in the margins.

"Since my lifetime can be divided into innumerable parts each of which is independent of the others, the fact that I existed a little while ago does not entail that I exist now, unless a cause 're-creates' me—or, in other words, preserves me—at this moment. For, when we attend to the nature of time, it's obvious that exactly the same power and action are required to preserve a thing at each moment through which it endures as would be required to create it anew if it had never existed. Hence, one of the things revealed by the light of nature is that preservation and creation differ only in the way we think of them.

"I ought to ask myself, then, whether I have the power to ensure that I, who now am, will exist in a little while. Since I am nothing but a thinking thing—or, at any rate, since I am now focusing on the part of me that thinks—I would surely be aware of this power if it were in me. But I find no such power. And from this I clearly see that there is an entity distinct from me on whom I depend."

The first proof for God's existence starts with the idea of God in Descartes' mind and shows that God must be the cause of this idea. The second proof of God's existence, which you just read, starts with Descartes' existence and shows that God must exist as the continuous re-creator of Descartes' existence. Because this proof is a bit more subtle that the first, I'm going to do most of the work.

Let us say I tried to refute Descartes by arguing that the pumping of my heart was the cause of my continuing to exist. He would simply point out that he is talking not about my life but about my whole existence. My heart causes my life to continue, but what causes my heart and everything else about me to continue to exist? Our hearts keep us alive, but what causes our hearts to continue in physical existence from one moment to the next? His answer would be that only God could be the cause of our continued existence.

Perhaps I could try to answer Descartes by saying that I myself am the cause of my own continued existence. I am typing this at 9:01 in the morning, and my existing at 9:01 in the morning causes me to continue to exist at 9:02 in the morning. Each moment of my life is an effect created by a previous cause, and that previous cause is the previous moment of my life. Therefore, God is not the cause of my continued existence, I am.

Descartes would probably answer that I really don't understand what it means for one thing to cause another. And perhaps he is right. When I move my fingers on the keyboard and cause the keys to move, my fingers are the cause and the movement of the keys is the effect. But for my fingers to cause the keys to move, my fingers and the keys *must exist at the same moment*. In fact, this is the case with all relations between a cause and an effect. When one thing causes another, the two must exist at the same moment. If A is said to cause B, they must meet at some particular moment; otherwise, it would be impossible for A to be the cause of B.

Take the simple case of two objects capable of motion. Let us say a

_____ rolls up to a _____ and causes the second object to move. The two objects must exist at the same moment of time for

one to affect the other, because if they didn't, _____

_____ . Descartes' point

seems to be that _____.
But how does this relate to his proof of God's existence?

He is arguing that only God and not we ourselves could be the cause of our continued existence. When I suggest that my existing at 9:01 is the cause of my existing at 9:02, he can refute this by pointing out that for one thing to have any effect on another, the two must exist *at the same time*. Thus, a self existing at 9:01 could not be the cause of the same self existing at 9:02 because the former obviously doesn't exist at the same time as the latter. Therefore, there must be something else that maintains the self in existence from one separate moment to the next, and that something Descartes goes on to define as God.

I am indebted to Ronald Rubin for drawing my attention to, and clarifying a key aspect of, Descartes' second proof for God's existence.

Thus, in *Meditation III*, Descartes offers two very different proofs of God's existence. In the first proof, Descartes analyzes his idea of God and discovers that this idea could have been caused only by God. In the second proof, Descartes analyzes the continuity of his, Descartes', existence and discovers that this continuity could have been maintained only by God.

Let's see how far we've come. Think back about what you learned about Descartes in the Introduction. Then look back through your notes for the first three Meditations. What is all this really about?

The main concepts in the Introduction were _____

_____

_____

_____

_____

In *Meditation I*, Descartes went through a long argument questioning his beliefs. He was seeking _____ .
He was even able to question whether he could be certain his body

was where it appeared to be by arguing _____

_____

_____ .

Then he imagined an all-powerful evil spirit so that _____

_____ .

In *Meditation II*, he established his first truth by showing that

_____ . In
addition, he carefully examined a piece of wax to demonstrate to

himself that _____

_____ .

Meditation III could be divided into two parts. In the first part, his most important points were _____

_____

_____ .

In the second part, his most important points were _____

_____

_____

_____ .

Now do one more task and then you can take a well-deserved rest. First, summarize Descartes' first proof of God's existence in no more than four sentences. Then, state the general idea of the second proof.

The first fact is _____

_____ .

The second fact is _____

_____ .

Add to this a third obvious fact that _____

_____

_____ .

And my fourth sentence is simply that from the above it is obvious that God must exist. However, learning from Descartes, I would offer this criticism of one of my first three sentences.

And that is that _____

_____

_____ .

Finally, what he seems to be arguing in the second proof of God's existence is _____

_____

_____

_____ .

Take your well-deserved rest.

MEDITATION IV

On Truth and Falsity

PREVIEW

Descartes begins with a summary of his progress toward perfect knowledge. Next, he establishes that God is no deceiver. But this raises a new problem. If God is no deceiver, a perfect being, how could He have created a being as imperfect as Descartes? Descartes answers this classic philosophical question by investigating the relationship between the mind's limited understanding and its unlimited will. Descartes concludes with a general principle for avoiding all errors.

MEDITATION IV

In this Meditation, continue to practice your annotation skills. Underline, circle, or number important points. Write paraphrases of key ideas in the margin.

In the last few days, I've gotten used to drawing my mind away from my senses. I've carefully noted that I really grasp very little about physical objects, that I know much more about the human mind, and that I know even more about God. Thus, I no longer find it hard to turn my thoughts away from things of which I can have mental images and toward things completely separate from matter, which I can only understand. Indeed, I have a much more distinct idea of the human mind, insofar as it is just a thinking thing that isn't extended in length, breadth, or depth and doesn't share anything else with physical objects, than I have of physical objects. And, when I note that I doubt or that I am incomplete and dependent, I have a clear and distinct idea of a complete and independent entity: God. From the fact that this idea is in me and that I who have the idea exist, I can clearly infer both that God exists and that I am completely dependent on Him for my existence from moment to moment. This is so obvious that I'm sure that people can't know anything more evidently or certainly. And it now seems to me that, from the contemplation of the true God in whom are hidden all treasures of knowledge and wisdom, there is a way to derive knowledge of other things.

In the first place, I know that it's impossible for Him ever to deceive me. Wherever there is fraud and deception, there is imperfection, and, while the ability to deceive may seem a sign of cunning or power, the desire to deceive reveals malice or weakness and hence is inconsistent with God's nature.

Next, I find in myself an ability to judge which, like everything else in me, I've gotten from God. Since He doesn't want to deceive me, He certainly hasn't given me an ability which will lead me wrong when properly used.

There could be no doubt about this—except that it may seem to imply that I don't err at all. For, if I've gotten everything in me from God and He

The difference between (a) God's power to deceive and (b) God's

desire to deceive is that (a) _____

_____ ,

whereas (b) _____

_____ .

60

hasn't given me the ability to err, it doesn't seem possible for me ever to err. Thus, as long as I think only of God and devote all my attention to Him, I can't find any cause for error and falsity. When I turn my attention back to myself, however, I find that I can make innumerable errors. In looking for the cause of these errors, I find before me, not just the real and positive idea of God, but also the negative idea of "nothingness"—the idea of that which is completely devoid of perfection. I find that I am "intermediate" between God and nothingness, between the supreme entity and nonentity. Insofar as I am the creation of the supreme entity, there's nothing in me to account for my being deceived or led into error, but, insofar as I somehow participate in nothingness or the nonentity—that is, insofar as I am distinct from the supreme entity itself and lack many things—it's not surprising that I go wrong. I thus understand that, in itself, error is a lack, rather than a real thing dependent on God. Hence, I understand that I can err without God's having given me a special ability to do so. Rather, I fall into error because my God-given ability to judge the truth is not infinite.

Descartes turns to a new problem. If God is a good God, how could He have created a being who makes errors?

Underline the key steps in Descartes' answer.

But there's still something to be explained. Error is not just an absence, but a deprivation—the lack of knowledge that somehow ought to be in me. But, when I attend to God's nature, it seems impossible that He's given me an ability that is an imperfect thing of its kind—an ability lacking a perfection that it ought to have. The greater the craftsman's skill, the more perfect his product. Then how can the supreme creator of all things have made something that isn't absolutely perfect? There's no doubt that God could have made me so that I never err and that He always wants what's best. Then is it better for me to err than not to err?

Descartes will eventually show it is better for him to be able to make errors. In the next paragraph, he

argues _____

_____

_____

_____

_____ .

When I pay more careful attention, I realize that I shouldn't be surprised at God's doing things that I can't explain. I shouldn't doubt His existence just because I find that I sometimes can't understand why or how He has made something. I know that my nature is weak and limited and that God's is limitless, incomprehensible, and infinite, and, from this, I can infer that He can do innumerable things whose reasons are unknown to me. On this ground alone, I regard the common practice of explaining things in terms of their purposes to be useless in physics: it would be foolhardy of me to think that I can discover God's purposes.

It also seems to me that, when asking whether God's works are perfect, I ought to look at all of them together, not at one in isolation. For something that seems imperfect when viewed alone might seem completely perfect when regarded as having a place in the world. Of course, since calling everything into doubt, I haven't established that anything exists besides me and God. But, when I consider God's immense power, I can't deny that He has made—or, in any case, that He could have made—many other things, and I must therefore view myself as having a place in a universe.

Next, turning to myself and investigating the nature of my errors (which are all that show me to be imperfect), I notice that these errors depend on two concurrent causes: my ability to know and my ability to choose freely—that is, my understanding and my will. But, with my understanding, I just grasp the ideas about which I form judgments, and error therefore cannot properly be said to arise from the understanding itself. While there may be innumerable things of which I have no idea, I can't say that I am deprived of these ideas, but only that I happen to lack them—for

His errors cannot come from his

understanding because _____

_____

_____

_____

_____ .

I don't have any reason to think that God ought to have given me a greater ability to know than He has. And, while I understand God to be a supremely skillful craftsman, I don't go on to think that He ought to endow each of his works with all the perfections that He can put in the others.

Nor can I complain about the scope or perfection of my God-given freedom of will—for I find that my will doesn't seem to me to be restricted in any way. Indeed, it seems well worth noting that nothing in me other than my will is so great and perfect that it couldn't conceivably be bigger or better. If I think about my ability to understand, for example, I realize that it is very small and restricted and I immediately form the idea of something much greater—indeed, of something supremely perfect and infinite. And, from the fact that I can form the idea of this thing, I infer that it is present in God's nature. Similarly, if I consider my other abilities, like the abilities to remember and to imagine, I clearly see that they all are weak and limited in me, but boundless in God. My will or freedom of choice is the only thing I find to be so great in me that I can't conceive of anything greater. In fact, it's largely for this reason that I regard myself as an image or likeness of God. God's will is incomparably greater than mine, of course, in virtue of the associated knowledge and power that make it stronger and more effective, and also in virtue of its greater range of objects. Yet, viewed in itself as a will, God's will seems no greater than mine. For having a will just amounts to being able either to do or not to do (affirm or deny, seek or avoid)—or, better, to being inclined to affirm or deny, seek or shun what the understanding offers, without any sense of being driven by external forces. To be free, I don't need to be inclined toward both alternatives. On the contrary, the more I lean toward one alternative—either because I understand the truth or goodness in it, or because God has so arranged my deepest thoughts—the more freely I choose it. Neither divine grace nor knowledge of nature ever diminishes my freedom; they increase and strengthen it. But the indifference that I experience when no consideration impels me toward one alternative over another is freedom of the lowest sort, whose presence reveals a defect or an absence of knowledge rather than a perfection. For, if I always knew what was good or true, I wouldn't ever deliberate about what to do or choose, and thus, though completely free, I would never be indifferent.

From this I see that my God-given ability to will is not itself the cause of my errors—for my will is great, a perfect thing of its kind. Neither is my power of understanding the cause of my errors; whenever I understand something, I understand it correctly and without the possibility of error, since my understanding comes from God. What then is the source of my errors? It is just that, while my will has a broader scope than my understanding, I don't keep it within the same bounds, but extend it to that which I don't understand. Being indifferent to these things, my will is easily led away from truth and goodness, and thus I am led into error and sin.

For example, I've asked for the last few days whether anything exists in the world, and I've noted that, from the fact that I ask this, it follows that I exist. I couldn't fail to judge that which I so clearly understood to be true. This wasn't because a force outside me compelled me to believe, but because an intense light in my understanding produced a strong inclination of my will. And, to the extent that I wasn't indifferent, I believed spontaneously and freely. However, while I now know that I exist insofar as I am a

The difference between Descartes' will and his other faculties, such as his understanding, is that his will is

_____

_____

_____ ,

whereas his other faculties are _____

_____

_____

_____

_____

_____ .

This paragraph is central to *Meditation IV.* He argues that his will is not the source of error because

_____

_____

_____ .

His understanding is not the source

of error because _____

_____

_____

_____ .

thinking thing, I notice in myself an idea of what it is to be a physical object and I come to wonder whether the thinking nature that's in me—or, rather, that *is* me—differs from this bodily nature or is identical to it. Nothing occurs to my reason (I am supposing) to convince me of one alternative rather than the other. Accordingly, I am completely indifferent to affirming either view, to denying either view, and even to suspending judgment.

And indifference of this sort is not limited to things of which the understanding is completely ignorant. It extends to everything about which the will deliberates in the absence of a sufficiently clear understanding. For, however strong the force with which plausible conjectures draw me toward one alternative, the knowledge that they are conjectures rather than assertions backed by certain and indubitable arguments is enough to push my assent the other way. The past few days have provided me with ample experience of this—for I am now supposing each of my former beliefs to be false just because I've found a way to call them into doubt.

If I suspend judgment when I don't clearly and distinctly grasp what's true, I obviously do right and am not deceived. But, if I either affirm or deny in a case of this sort, I misuse my freedom of choice. If I affirm what is false, I clearly err, and, if I stumble onto the truth, I'm still blameworthy since the light of nature reveals that a perception of the understanding should always precede a decision of the will. In these misuses of freedom of choice lies the deprivation that accounts for error. And this deprivation, I maintain, lies in the working of the will insofar as it comes from me—not in my God-given ability to will, or even in the will's operation insofar as it derives from Him.

I have no reason to complain that God hasn't given me a more perfect understanding or a greater natural light than He has. It's in the nature of a finite understanding that there are many things it can't understand, and it's in the nature of created understanding that it's finite. Indeed, I ought to be grateful to Him who owes me absolutely nothing for what He has bestowed, rather than taking myself to be deprived or robbed of what God hasn't given me.

And I have no reason to complain about God's having given me a will whose scope is greater than my understanding's. The will is like a unity made of inseparable parts; its nature apparently will not allow anything to be taken away from it. And, really, the wider the scope of my will, the more grateful I ought to be to Him who gave it to me.

Finally, I ought not to complain that God concurs in bringing about the acts of will and judgment in which I err. Insofar as these acts derive from God, they are completely true and good, and I am more perfect with the ability to perform these acts than I would be without it. And, the deprivation that is the real ground of falsity and error doesn't need God's concurrence, since it's not a thing. When we regard God as its cause, we should say that it is an absence rather than a deprivation. For it clearly is no imperfection in God that He has given me the freedom to assent or not to assent to things of which He hasn't given me a clear and distinct grasp. Rather, it is undoubtedly an imperfection in me that I misuse this freedom by passing judgment on things that I don't properly understand. I see, of course, that God could easily have brought it about that, while I remain free and limited in knowledge, I never err: He could have implanted in me a clear and distinct understanding of everything about which I was ever going to make a

The source of error must be _____

_____

_____

_____

because _____

_____

_____

_____ .

Underline all the reasons why Descartes cannot blame God for human errors.

The main reasons he cannot blame God for human error are

_____

_____

_____

_____

_____

_____

_____

_____ .

choice, or He could have indelibly impressed on my memory that I must never pass judgment on something that I don't clearly and distinctly understand. And I also understand that, regarded in isolation from everything else, I would have been more perfect if God had made me so that I never err. But I can't deny that, because some things are immune to error while others are not, the universe is more perfect than it would have been if all its parts were alike. And I have no right to complain about God's wanting me to hold a place in the world other than the greatest and most perfect.

Besides, if I can't avoid error by having a clear grasp of every matter on which I make a choice, I can avoid it in the other way, which only requires remembering that I must not pass judgment on matters whose truth isn't apparent. For, although I find myself too weak to fix my attention permanently on this single thought, I can—by careful and frequent meditation—ensure that I call it to mind whenever it's needed and thus that I acquire the habit of avoiding error.

Since the first and foremost perfection of man lies in avoiding error, I've profited from today's meditation, in which I've investigated the cause of error and falsity. Clearly, the only possible cause of error is the one I have described. When I limit my will's range of judgment to the things presented clearly and distinctly to my understanding, I obviously cannot err—for everything that I clearly and distinctly grasp is something and hence must come, not from nothing, but from God—God, I say, who is supremely perfect and who cannot possibly deceive. Therefore, what I clearly and distinctly grasp is unquestionably true. Today, then, I have learned what to avoid in order not to err and also what to do to reach the truth. I surely will reach the truth if I just attend to the things that I understand perfectly and distinguish them from those that I grasp more obscurely and confusedly. And that's what I'll take care to do from now on.

Descartes can avoid error by

_____

_____

_____ .

THINKING ABOUT MEDITATION IV

Begin in the same way as before by describing the major points Descartes covered.

The major concepts Descartes discussed were _____

_____

_____

_____ .

Now try your hand at criticism. Select a few sentences and restate them in your own words to demonstrate that you understand exactly what Descartes is saying. Then present an argument against their truth.

Descartes makes one of his weakest points in *Meditation IV* when

he says, " _____

_____

_____ ."

Putting this into my own words, _____

_____

_____ .

I will offer two arguments against what he says. First, he cannot

be right because _____

_____

_____ .

An example of what I mean is _____

_____

_____ .

My second argument is _____

_____

_____ .

An example of what I mean is _____

_____

_____ .

Here, at the end of one long sentence, Descartes summarizes a version of his proof of God's existence.

"And, when I note that I doubt or that I am incomplete and dependent, I have a clear and distinct idea of a complete and independent entity: God. From the fact that this idea is in me and that I who have the idea exist, I can clearly infer both that God exists and that I am completely dependent on Him for my existence from moment to moment. This is so obvious that I'm sure that people can't know anything more evidently or certainly."

Try putting the main idea here in your own words, and then we will talk about it.

What Descartes is saying about himself is _____

_____ . What he is saying about

God is _____ . From the

difference between these two, he argues that God must exist

because _____

_____ .

Descartes argues that he could not know he was an imperfect being if he did not already know what a perfect being was. When he doubts, he comes face to face with his imperfection. But how would he know what imperfection was, if he did not have an inborn standard of perfection (God) to measure his imperfection with? For example, let us say I ask you if you live a furlong from school.

If I said I didn't live a furlong from school, that would imply I knew what a _____ was. A better example would be this: If I said _____ , that would clearly imply I knew what _____ was; otherwise, I couldn't make the statement. When Descartes says he is a _____ being, he could only make this statement if he knew the *opposite*, what a _____ being was. Therefore, from this he can prove that _____ exists because _____

_____ .

In this Meditation, Descartes addresses one of the great problems of Christian philosophy. If God exists and is perfect, why or how could he have created such imperfect creatures? How would you answer this question?

A good question. Some examples of the serious imperfections of humans are _____

_____ .

In my own life, I can certainly see imperfections whenever I

_____ .

If I were trying to say how a perfect God could have made such an imperfect creature, I would say _____

_____ because _____

_____ .

The problem would be similar to showing how an imperfect work of art could have come from the hand of an artist who never makes mistakes. God is the artist who is said never to make mistakes. There seems to be an obvious contradiction. It appears we have to say one of two things:

1. God is not perfect, and that is why we are not perfect.
2. God is perfect, and we are also somehow perfect.

But both 1 and 2 appear to be unacceptable to Christianity.

Christians would disagree with 1 because _____

_____ . And, especially according to the story of Adam and Eve, they would also disagree with 2 because _____

_____ .

Read Descartes' account of error and the source of our imperfections, and then I will explain his whole position more fully.

"What then is the source of my errors? It is just that, while my will has a broader scope than my understanding, I don't keep it within the same bounds, but extend it to that which I don't understand. Being indifferent to these things, my will is easily led away from truth and goodness, and thus I am lead into error and sin."

Try thinking this through from Descartes' point of view.

My mind has two faculties: will and understanding. For example, I exercise an act of will when I _____ . I perform an act of understanding when I "clearly and distinctly" conceive of _____ . However, Descartes says the will "has a broader scope than my understanding. . . ." He means _____ . Therefore, I commit errors when I use the will and the understanding incorrectly. An example would be my deciding with my will to _____ _____ . In this case, my understanding _____ _____ . A correct use of will and understanding in this particular case would be _____ _____ .

In *Meditation IV,* Descartes says in effect that God made both the will and the understanding as perfect as each one could be. Since he was creating a finite creature, the understanding in such a creature would of necessity be finite, limited. On the other hand, will can be either free or not free. Descartes would argue that it is clearly more perfect to have a free will than a will that is not free. Therefore, God made us as perfect as possible: finite understanding coupled to a free will. Thus, we can decide to do things that we do not fully understand, and we fall into errors. An example?

An example would be my exercising my will to _____ _____ . But my understanding is limited to _____ . Therefore, I fall into error because _____ .

Descartes goes on to say that in effect we fall into error only because we use God's perfect gifts imperfectly. If we limit our will to what we "clearly and distinctly" understand, we can never fall into error. What do you think of this entire argument?

The argument could be divided into four parts: a description of will, a description of understanding, a description of how these two produce human error, a description of how these two are related to a perfect God. The strength of Descartes' description of the will is _____

_____ .

A weakness is _____

_____ .

The strength of Descartes' description of the understanding is

_____ .

A weakness is _____

_____ .

Reviewing what you said, the incorrect application of will and

understanding produces error because _____

_____ .

A strength of this view is _____

_____ .

A weakness is _____

_____ .

In essence, Descartes argues that God is still perfect even though his

creations make mistakes because _____

_____

_____ .

The strongest part of his entire argument is _____

_____ . My reason for saying this is _____

_____ .

The weakest part of his entire argument is _____

_____ . My reason for saying this is _____

_____ . Now I
have a hard question for you. You said that one has to say one of
two things:

1. God is not perfect, and that is why we are not perfect.
2. God is perfect, and we are also somehow perfect.

Which does Descartes agree with?

Perhaps Descartes would change 2 to "God is perfect, and we are as
perfect as we need to be to avoid errors."

Before you go further, sum up the key points Descartes has established in the first four Meditations.

Key points in *Meditation I:* _____

_____

_____

_____

_____ .

Key points in *Meditation II:* _____

_____

_____

_____

_____ .

Key points in *Meditation III:* _____

_____

_____

_____

_____ .

Key points in *Meditation IV:* _____

_____

_____

_____

_____

_____ .

Exercise 4.1

Number the following ideas in the order in which Descartes introduces them in *Meditation IV.*

a. Errors come from not keeping the will within the bounds of clear understanding.

b. Descartes is midway between God and nothingness.

c. By thinking about God, Descartes can discover other truths.

d. Errors are somehow produced by the interaction of two causes, the will and the understanding.

e. It is not possible for God to deceive Descartes.

f. Descartes' will is perfect in that, like God's will, it is free.

Exercise 4.2

Though it may occasionally be difficult to find, underline the conclusion in the following arguments. When in doubt, consult the context in the Meditation where the argument occurs and ask yourself which statement Descartes is most interested in proving. That statement will be the conclusion.

a. "Since He doesn't want to deceive me, He certainly hasn't given me an ability which will lead me wrong when properly used."

b. The will, to be a will, could not be less than it is. No parts can be removed from the will. Descartes cannot criticize God for giving him a will that is broader than his understanding.

c. God has nothing to do with Descartes' making mistakes. Descartes makes mistakes because he "somehow participate[s] in nothingness."

d. Descartes cannot criticize God for not giving him a better understanding. A limited being like Descartes will have a limited understanding.

e. Descartes has a limited nature. God can do things that Descartes will never understand. God has an infinite nature.

f. It is not possible to be a deceiver. Deception implies imperfection. God is not imperfect.

g. A free will is a free will. Descartes' will, though linked to a less powerful understanding than God's, is just as free as God's will.

Exercise 4.3

Arrange the arguments in 4.2 in the same order in which they occur in *Meditation IV*.

Exercise 4.4

Carefully read the following arguments from *Meditation IV*.

1. "[1] In the first place, I know that it's impossible for Him ever to deceive me. [2] Wherever there is fraud and deception, there is imperfection, and, [3] while the ability to deceive may seem a sign of cunning or power, the desire to deceive reveals malice or weakness and [4] hence is inconsistent with God's nature."
   a. What is "inconsistent with God's nature"?
   b. Which of the following are true?
      1. 1 and 2 are offered to support 3.
      2. 2 and 3 are offered to support 4.
      3. 1, 2, and 3 are offered to support 4.

    c. According to this argument, why is God not a deceiver?

    d. According to this argument, which of the following are true?

       1. If you have imperfection, then you have fraud and deception.

       2. If you have fraud and deception, then you have imperfection.

       3. The ability to deceive could not be consistent with cunning or power.

       4. God has no ability to deceive.

2. "[1] Insofar as I am the creation of the supreme entity, [2] there's nothing in me to account for my being deceived or led into error, [3] but, insofar as I somehow participate in nothingness or the nonentity—that is, insofar as I am distinct from the supreme entity itself and lack many things—it's not surprising that I go wrong. [4] I thus understand that, in itself, error is a lack, rather than a real thing dependent on God. [5] Hence, I understand that I can err without God's having given me a special ability to do so. [6] Rather, I fall into error because my God-given ability to judge the truth is not infinite."

    a. Is 2 a conclusion supported by the evidence of 1 or vice versa?

    b. According to which statement[s] does error exist in Descartes?

    c. According to which statement[s] does error not exist in Descartes?

    d. According to Descartes' argument, how can error both exist and not exist?

MEDITATION V

On the Essence of Material Objects and More on God's Existence

PREVIEW

Descartes explores his ideas of physical objects and offers an argument that he couldn't have invented these ideas. Next, by demonstrating that God's existence is inextricably linked to His essence, Descartes offers his last proof for God's existence. Carefully examining God's essence reveals to Descartes that God must exist. Just as the concept of a valley is hidden within the concept of a mountain, so the concept of God's existence is hidden within the concept of His essence. This proof confirms Descartes' faith that he can be certain of "what I grasp clearly and distinctly."

MEDITATION V

Many questions remain about God's attributes and about the nature of my self or mind. I may return to these questions later. But now, having found what to do and what to avoid in order to attain truth, I regard nothing as more pressing than to work my way out of the doubts that I raised the other day and to see whether I can find anything certain about material objects.

But, before asking whether any such objects exist outside me, I ought to consider the ideas of these objects as they exist in my thoughts and see which are clear and which confused.

I have a distinct mental image of the quantity that philosophers commonly call continuous. That is, I have a distinct mental image of the extension of this quality—or rather of the quantified thing—in length, breadth, and depth. I can distinguish various parts of this thing. I can ascribe various sizes, shapes, places, and motions to these parts and various durations to the motions.

In addition to having a thorough knowledge of extension in general, I grasp innumerable particulars about things like shape, number, and motion, when I pay careful attention. The truth of these particulars is so obvious and so consonant with my nature that, when I first think of one of these things, I seem not so much to be learning something novel as to be remembering something that I already knew—or noticing for the first time something that had long been in me without my having turned my mind's eye toward it.

What's important here, I think, is that I find in myself innumerable ideas of things which, though they may not exist outside me, can't be said to be nothing. While I have some control over my thoughts of these things, I do not make the things up: they have their own real and immutable natures. Suppose, for example, that I have a mental image of a triangle. While it may be that no figure of this sort does exist or ever has existed outside my thought, the figure has a fixed nature (essence or form), immutable and eternal, which hasn't been produced by me and isn't dependent on my mind. The proof is that I can demonstrate various propositions about the triangle, such as that its angles equal two right angles and that its greatest side subtends its greatest angle. Even though I didn't think of these propositions at all when I first imagined the triangle, I now clearly see their truth whether I want to or not, and it follows that I didn't make them up.

It isn't relevant that, having seen triangular physical objects, I may have gotten the idea of the triangle from external objects through my organs of sense. For I can think of innumerable other figures whose ideas I could not conceivably have gotten through my senses, and I can demonstrate facts about these other figures just as I can about the triangle. Since I know these facts clearly, they must be true, and they therefore must be something rather than nothing. For it's obvious that everything true is something, and, as I have shown, everything that I know clearly and distinctly is true. But, even if I hadn't shown this, the nature of my mind would have made it impossible for me to withhold my assent from these things, at least when I clearly and distinctly grasped them. As I recall, even when I clung most tightly to objects of sense, I regarded truths about shape and number—truths of arithmetic, geometry, and pure mathematics—as more certain than any others.

Descartes' main point about triangles and other geometric figures is _____ _____ _____ _____ _____ .

But, if anything whose idea I can draw from my thought must in fact have everything that I clearly and distinctly grasp it to have, can't I derive from this a proof of God's existence? Surely, I find the idea of God, a supremely perfect being, in me no less clearly than I find the ideas of figures and numbers. And I understand as clearly and distinctly that eternal existence belongs to His nature as that the things which I demonstrate of a figure or number belong to the nature of the figure or number. Accordingly, even if what I have thought up in the past few days hasn't been entirely true, I ought to be at least as certain of God's existence as I used to be of the truths of pure mathematics.

Underline the key steps in this new proof of God's existence.

At first, this reasoning may seem unclear and fallacious. Since I'm accustomed to distinguishing existence from essence in other cases, I find it easy to convince myself that I can separate God's existence from His essence and hence that I can think of God as nonexistent. But, when I pay more careful attention, it's clear that I can no more separate God's existence from His essence than a triangle's angles equaling two right angles from the essence of the triangle, or the idea of a valley from the idea of a mountain. It's no less impossible to think that God (the supremely perfect being) lacks existence (a perfection) than to think that a mountain lacks a valley.

God is to His _____ as a mountain is to _____ because _____ _____ _____ _____ _____ .

Well, suppose that I can't think of God without existence, just as I can't think of a mountain without a valley. From the fact that I can think of a mountain with a valley, it doesn't follow that a mountain exists in the world. Similarly, from the fact that I can think of God as existing, it doesn't seem to follow that He exists. For my thought doesn't impose any necessity on things. It may be that, just as I can imagine a winged horse when no such horse exists, I can ascribe existence to God when no God exists.

Compare Descartes' proof of God's existence with Anselm's proof in Appendix A.

Here Descartes offers a

counterargument. The point is _____

_____

_____ .

He answers the counterargument by

attempting to show _____

_____

_____

_____

_____ .

Write a good, descriptive title for each of the following five paragraphs.

1. _____

_____

_____

No, there is a fallacy here. From the fact that I can't think of a mountain without a valley it follows, not that the mountain and valley exist, but only that whether they exist or not they can't be separated from one another. But, from the fact that I can't think of God without existence, it follows that existence is inseparable from Him and hence that He really exists. It's not that my thoughts make it so or impose a necessity on things. On the contrary, it's the fact that God does exist that necessitates my thinking of Him as I do. For I am not free to think of God without existence—of the supremely perfect being without supreme perfection—as I am free to think of a horse with or without wings.

Now someone might say this: "If I take God to have all perfections, and if I take existence to be a perfection, I must take God to exist, but I needn't accept the premise that God has all perfections. Similarly, if I accept the premise that every quadrilateral can be inscribed in a circle, I'm forced to the patently false view that every rhombus can be inscribed in a circle, but I need not accept the premise." But this should not be said. For, while it's not necessary that the idea of God occurs to me, it is necessary that, whenever I think of the primary and supreme entity and bring the idea of Him out of my mind's "treasury," I attribute all perfections to Him, even if I don't enumerate them or consider them individually. And this necessity ensures that, when I do notice that existence is a perfection, I can rightly conclude that the primary and supreme being exists. Similarly, while it's not necessary that I ever imagine a triangle, it is necessary that, when I do choose to consider a rectilinear figure having exactly three angles, I attribute to it properties from which I can rightly infer that its angles are no more than two right angles, perhaps without noticing that I am doing so. But, when I consider which shapes can be inscribed in the circle, there's absolutely no necessity for my thinking that all quadrilaterals are among them. Indeed, I can't even think that all quadrilaterals are among them, since I've resolved to accept only what I clearly and distinctly understand. Thus my false suppositions differ greatly from the true ideas implanted in me, the first and foremost of which is my idea of God. In many ways, I see that this idea is not a figment of my thought, but the image of a real and immutable nature. For one thing, God is the only thing that I can think of whose existence belongs to its essence. For another thing, I can't conceive of there being two or more such Gods, and, having supposed that one God now exists, I see that He has necessarily existed from all eternity and will continue to exist into eternity. And I also perceive many other things in God that I can't diminish or alter.

But, whatever proof I offer, it always comes back to the fact that I am only convinced of what I grasp clearly and distinctly. Of the things that I grasp in this way, some are obvious to everyone. Some are discovered only by those who examine things more closely and search more carefully, but, once these things have been discovered, they are regarded as no less certain than the others. That the square on the hypotenuse of a right triangle equals the sum of the squares on the other sides is not as readily apparent as that the hypotenuse subtends the greatest angle, but, once it has been seen, it is believed just as firmly. And, when I'm not overwhelmed by prejudices and my thoughts aren't besieged by images of sensible things, there surely is nothing that I know earlier or more easily than facts about God. For what is more self-evident than there is a supreme entity—that God, the only thing whose existence belongs to His essence, exists?

While I need to pay careful attention in order to grasp this, I'm now as certain of it as of anything that seems most certain. In addition, I now see that the certainty of everything else so depends on it that, if I weren't certain of it, I couldn't know anything perfectly.

Of course, my nature is such that, when I grasp something clearly and distinctly, I can't fail to believe it. But my nature is also such that I can't permanently fix my attention on a single thing so as always to grasp it clearly, and memories of previous judgments often come to me when I am no longer attending to the grounds on which I originally made them. Accordingly, if I were ignorant of God, arguments could be produced that would easily overthrow my opinions, and I therefore would have unstable and changing opinions rather than true and certain knowledge. For example, when I consider the nature of the triangle, it seems plain to me—steeped as I am in the principles of geometry—that its three angles equal two right angles: I can't fail to believe this as long as I pay attention to its demonstration. But, if I were ignorant of God, I might come to doubt its truth as soon as my mind's eye turned away from its demonstration, even if I recalled having once grasped it clearly. For I could convince myself that I've been so constructed by nature that I sometimes err about what I believe myself to grasp most plainly—especially if I remembered that, having taken many things to be true and certain, I had later found grounds on which to judge them false.

But now I grasp that God exists, and I understand both that everything else depends on Him and that He's not a deceiver. From this, I infer that everything I clearly and distinctly grasp must be true. Even if I no longer pay attention to the grounds on which I judged God to exist, my recollection that I once clearly and distinctly knew Him to exist ensures that no contrary ground can be produced to push me towards doubt. About God's existence, I have true and certain knowledge. And I have such knowledge, not just about this one thing, but about everything else that I remember having proven, like the theorems of geometry. For what can now be said against my believing these things? That I am so constructed that I always err? But I now know that I can't err about what I clearly understand. That much of what I took to be true and certain I later found to be false? But I didn't grasp any of these things clearly and distinctly; ignorant of the true standard of truth, I based my belief on grounds that I later found to be unsound. Then what can be said? What about the objection (which I recently used against myself) that I may be dreaming and that the things I'm now experiencing may be as unreal as those that occur to me in sleep? No, even this is irrelevant. For, even if I am dreaming, everything that is evident to my understanding must be true.

Thus I plainly see that the certainty and truth of all my knowledge derives from one thing: my thought of the true God. Before I knew Him, I couldn't know anything else perfectly. But now I can plainly and certainly know innumerable things, not only about God and other mental beings, but also about the nature of physical objects, insofar as it is the subject matter of pure mathematics.

2. _____

_____

_____

3. _____

_____

_____

4. _____

_____

_____

5. _____

_____

_____

THINKING ABOUT MEDITATION V

What were Descartes' main topics in this Meditation?

I would say they were _____

_____

_____

_____ .

In this section, we will confine our attention to Descartes' new proof of God's existence. Recall that the first proof went something like this:

1. Descartes has an idea of God, a perfect being.

2. This idea must have a cause . . . it must have come from somewhere.

3. Descartes could not be the cause of the idea because he is an imperfect being and an imperfect being could not be the cause of the idea of a perfect God. . . . (That would be a case of an effect, the idea of a perfect God, being greater than its cause, an imperfect being.)

4. Therefore, God must exist as the cause of Descartes' idea of God.

Now, compare your proof of God's existence on pages 10–11 with points 1–4 above. Here is a different proof (the third and last in the *Meditations*) for God's existence that Descartes offers in *Meditation V.*

"[1] Since I'm accustomed to distinguishing existence from essence in other cases, I find it easy to convince myself that I can separate God's existence from His essence and hence that I can think of God as nonexistent. [2] But, when I pay more careful attention, it's clear that I can no more separate God's existence from His essence than a triangle's angles equaling two right angles from the essence of the triangle, or the idea of a valley from the idea of a mountain. [3] It's no less impossible to think that God (the supremely perfect being) lacks existence (a perfection) than to think that a mountain lacks a valley."

Try this on your own and then I will guide you through it.

In 1, he is saying _____

_____ .

In 2, he is saying _____

_____ .

For example, the essence of a square might be _____

_____ ,

and the point he is making about the relationship between essence

and existence as applied to a square would be _____

_____ . And this is *different* from

the case with God because _____

_____ .

In 3, he says _____

_____

_____ .

In his first proof for God's existence, Descartes began with his own idea of God. In the second proof, he began with his own existence. In this third proof, he tries to consider God's nature directly. To understand the third proof, let's talk about two important words in philosophy: *essence* and *existence.* The terms probably came to Descartes from Thomas Aquinas, perhaps the greatest of the Medieval philosophers. Take your example of a square. Part of the essence of a square is that it has four equal and parallel sides, and what distinguishes its essence from the essence of a parallelogram is that each inner angle of the square is a right angle. Note that when you describe the essence of a square, you do not have to say anything about whether any particular square exists. Its essence, four-equal-sidedness-with-four-right-interior-angles, would still be the essence of a square even if all squares vanished from the world. Squares have an essence that is not tied to their existence.

Let us say I am looking at a circle on the blackboard. Its essence as

a circle might be defined as _____

_____ . If I erase the circle, I have changed this particular circle. It no longer exists. But the essence of a circle is not changed. In the case of circles, squares, or triangles, I could generalize by saying the relationship between essence and

existence is _____

_____ .

Let's continue. Imagine we divided everything that exists into two piles. In one pile (A) we have things whose existence was not part of their essence, and in the other pile (B) we have things whose existence could not be divided from their essence.

If Descartes described the kinds of things in pile A, he would find

_____

_____ .

I've got a feeling that there would be only one item in pile B, and

that would be _____ .

I have a feeling you had the right feeling. Think for a second about God as Descartes would. God is defined as a perfect being. He is not nearly perfect, or almost perfect, but completely perfect. God is a being "than whom none greater can be conceived," as Anselm would say. If He is a perfect being, the greatest that can be conceived, He must certainly have all perfections. Existence is a perfection. All perfections are part of God's essence. Therefore, God's essence is linked to His existence and therefore He must exist. As Descartes says:

". . . I am not free to think of God without existence—of the supremely perfect being without supreme perfection—as I am free to think of a horse with or without wings."

Try to think about God as Descartes would.

I am thinking about a horse right now. I can add wings to it. I can take the wings away. Then thinking of the terms *existence* and *essence*, I must say that in the case of a horse, wings are not part of its

_____

_____ .

Or take the case of a ball. I am thinking of a ball right now. I can make it red or blue, and it is still a ball. Therefore, color is not part

of a ball's _____ . However, let me think of a square. Whenever I think of a square, I must think of it as having four equal sides. Thinking of the terms *essence* and *existence*, I must say that four equal sides is definitely part of the square's

_____ . Descartes wants to say that square is to four-

sidedness as _____ is to God's _____ .

When I think of a perfect being, I must find its _____

as part of its essence because _____

_____

_____ .

If someone asks you what you did today, you can reply that you created a twentieth-century version of Descartes' seventeenth-century version of Anselm's eleventh-century ontological argument.

Let me sum up for you. Just as it is impossible "clearly and distinctly" to conceive of a square without four straight, equal sides or a mountain range without valleys, it is impossible to conceive of God, a perfect being, as not existing. When one thinks of a perfect being as not existing, one is trying to think of a perfect being who is not perfect, who lacks the supreme perfection of existence. This is like trying to think of a square with unequal sides.

Exercise 5.1

Decide whether each of the following is a *Pro* argument or a *Con* argument. Then number the *Pro* arguments and the *Con* arguments in the order in which they occur in *Meditation V*. (Remember, we have defined *Pro* arguments as those that take Descartes closer to his goal of certitude and *Con* arguments as those that take him further away. Beginning with the first *Pro* argument, every *Pro* argument should be followed by a *Con* argument.)

a. God doesn't necessarily have all perfections; therefore, He need not have the perfection of existence.

b. God's existence is as attached to His essence as a mountain is attached to a valley.

c. The supreme being must have all perfections. Existence is a perfection. Therefore, God has the perfection of existence.

d. Because in other cases existence is not part of essence, God's existence is not necessarily part of His essence.

e. Just as it is no proof that a mountain exists simply because one can't think of a mountain without a valley, in the same way, it is no proof that God exists simply because one can't think of God without His existence.

f. Eternal existence is as much a part of God's essence as any characteristic that can be derived from a number or a shape.

g. Because one can't think of God without thinking of His existence, God does exist. Mountains must have valleys, whether or not mountains exist.

Exercise 5.2

Carefully read paragraph 5 ("What's important here . . ."). Pay special attention to the last two sentences ("The proof is that . . ." and "Even though . . .").

1. "What's important here" is that
   a. Descartes' ideas "may not exist outside me."
   b. Descartes' ideas "can't be said to be nothing."
   c. Descartes finds in himself "innumerable ideas of things."

2. The "proof" is a proof that
   a. Triangles exist in the physical world.
   b. No triangles exist in the physical world.
   c. The idea of a triangle, because of the complex properties it has, could have been invented by Descartes.
   d. If Descartes had invented his idea of a triangle, the triangle wouldn't have the complex properties it has.

Exercise 5.3

Carefully read paragraph 8 ("At first, this reasoning . . ."). Check the correct statements.

1. "This reasoning" in the first sentence refers to the fact that Descartes should be as certain of God's existence as he is of mathematical truths.

2. The paragraph contains one argument against God's existence and one argument for God's existence.

3. The paragraph contains two arguments against God's existence.

4. The paragraph contains two arguments for God's existence.

5. Just as one can mentally separate a mountain from a valley, so one can mentally separate God's existence from His essence.

6. God's existence is to His essence as a mountain is to a valley.

Exercise 5.4

Carefully read paragraph 9 ("Well, suppose that I can't . . ."). Check the correct statements.

1. Just because it's impossible to think of God without existence, that doesn't prove that God exists.

2. Just because mountains can't exist without valleys, that doesn't prove that mountains exist in the world.

3. Imagining a winged horse when no winged horse exists is used as evidence to show that God's existence can be thought of without His essence.

4. Imagining a winged horse when no winged horse exists is used as evidence to show that thinking that God must exist doesn't prove that God does exist.

5. Just as a winged horse can be imagined as separate from an actually existing horse, God's existence can be imagined as separate from His actual essence.

Exercise 5.5

Carefully read paragraph 10 ("No, there is a fallacy here . . ."). Check the correct statements.

1. Descartes agrees that he hasn't proved that God exists.

2. Because Descartes thinks of God existing, God must exist.

3. Because God exists, Descartes must think of Him as existing.

4. It is not possible to think of God's essence without thinking of His existence.

5. Just as Descartes can think of a horse with or without wings, he can think of God with or without existence.

MEDITATION VI

~

On the Existence of Material Objects and the Real Distinction of Mind from Body

PREVIEW

Descartes continues to explore his ideas of physical objects. Distinguishing between "having a mental image and having a pure understanding," he deduces that some of his mental images "probably" come from actual physical objects. To become more certain, he makes a three-part examination of his senses. First, he reviews what, before his *Meditations*, he believed his senses told him. Second, he reexamines his grounds for doubting his senses. Third, he investigates his senses and concludes that because God is no deceiver, Descartes must believe that his senses do not deceive him about the existence of physical objects.

To further clear God of any charge of deception, Descartes considers the special occasions when our God-given "natural impulses" guide us toward what is harmful. He concludes his *Meditations* by describing a technique for avoiding all sense error and distinguishing dreaming from waking.

MEDITATION VI

It remains for me to examine whether material objects exist. Insofar as they are the subject of pure mathematics, I now know at least that they can exist, because I grasp them clearly and distinctly. For God can undoubtedly make whatever I can grasp in this way, and I never judge that something is impossible for Him to make unless there would be a contradiction in my grasping the thing distinctly. Also, the fact that I find myself having mental images when I turn my attention to physical objects seems to imply that these objects really do exist. For, when I pay careful attention to what it is to have a mental image, it seems to me that it's just the application of my power of thought to a certain body which is immediately present to it and which must therefore exist.

To clarify this, I'll examine the difference between having a mental image and having a pure understanding. When I have a mental image of a triangle, for example, I don't just understand that it is a figure bounded by three lines; I also "look at" the lines as though they were present to my mind's eye. And this is what I call having a mental image. When I want to think of a chiliagon, I understand that it is a figure with a thousand sides as well as I understand that a triangle is a figure with three, but I can't imagine its sides or "look" at them as though they were present. Being accustomed to using images when I think about physical objects, I may confusedly picture some figure to myself,

There are no annotation aids in this Meditation. Practice what you have learned by adding your own. Circle, number, and/or underline key points. Paraphrase Descartes in the margin. Write titles for paragraphs, create your own examples of what Descartes is arguing, and carefully reread key passages. Think with Descartes.

but this figure obviously is not a chiliagon—for it in no way differs from what I present to myself when thinking about a myriagon or any other many-sided figure, and it doesn't help me to discern the properties that distinguish chiliagons from other polygons. If it's a pentagon that is in question, I can understand its shape, as I can that of the chiliagon, without the aid of mental images. But I can also get a mental image of the pentagon by directing my mind's eye to its five lines and to the area that they bound. And it's obvious to me that getting this mental image requires a special mental effort different from that needed for understanding—a special effort which clearly reveals the difference between having a mental image and having a pure understanding.

It also seems to me that my power of having mental images, being distinct from my power of understanding, is not essential to my self or, in other words, to my mind—for, if I were to lose this ability, I would surely remain the same thing that I now am. And it seems to follow that this ability depends on something distinct from me. If we suppose that there is a body so associated with my mind that the mind can "look into" it at will, it's easy to understand how my mind might get mental images of physical objects by means of my body. If there were such a body, the mode of thinking that we call imagination would differ from pure understanding in only one way: when the mind understood something, it would turn "inward" and view an idea that it found in itself, but, when it had mental images, it would turn to the body and look at something there which resembled an idea that it had understood by itself or had grasped by sense. As I've said, then, it's easy to see how I get mental images, if we supposed that my body exists. And, since I don't have in mind any other equally plausible explanation of my ability to have mental images, I conjecture that physical objects probably do exist. But this conjecture is only probable. Despite my careful and thorough investigation, the distinct idea of bodily nature that I get from mental images does not seem to have anything in it from which the conclusion that physical objects exist validly follows.

Besides having a mental image of the bodily nature that is the subject matter of pure mathematics, I have mental images of things which are not so distinct—things like colors, sounds, flavors, and pains. But I seem to grasp these things better by sense, from which they seem to come (with the aid of memory) to the understanding. Thus, to deal with these things more fully, I must examine the senses and see whether there is anything in the mode of awareness that I call sensation from which I can draw a conclusive argument for the existence of physical objects.

First, I'll remind myself of the things that I believed really to be as I perceived them and of the grounds for my belief. Next, I'll set out the grounds on which I later called this belief into doubt. And, finally, I'll consider what I ought to think now.

To begin with, I sensed that I had a head, hands, feet, and the other members that make up a human body. I viewed this body as part, or maybe even as all, of me. I sensed that it was influenced by other physical objects whose effects could be either beneficial or harmful. I judged these effects to be beneficial to the extent that I felt pleasant sensations and harmful to the extent that I felt pain. And, in addition to sensations of pain and pleasure, I sensed hunger, thirst, and other such desires—and also bodily inclinations towards cheerfulness, sadness, and other emotions. Outside me, I sensed, not just extension, shape, and motion, but also hardness, hotness, and other qualities detected by touch. I also sensed light, color, odor, taste, and sound—qualities by whose variation I distinguished such things as the sky, earth, and sea from one another.

In view of these ideas of qualities (which presented themselves to my thought and were all that I really sensed directly), I had some reason for believing that I sensed objects distinct from my thought—physical objects from which the ideas came. For I found that these ideas came to me independently of my desires so that, however much I tried, I couldn't sense an object when it wasn't present to an organ of sense or fail to sense one when it was present. And, since the ideas that I grasped by sense were much livelier, more explicit, and (in their own way) more distinct than those I deliberately created or found impressed in my memory, it seemed that these ideas could not have come from me and thus that they came from something else. Having no conception of these things other than that suggested by my sensory ideas, I could only think that the things resembled the ideas. Indeed, since I remembered using my senses before my reason, since I found the ideas that I created in myself to be less explicit than those grasped by sense, and since I found the ideas that I created to be composed largely of those that I had grasped by sense, I easily convinced myself that I didn't understand anything at all unless I had first sensed it.

I also had some reason for supporting that a certain physical object, which I viewed as belonging to me in a special way, was related to me more closely than any other. I couldn't be separated from it as I could from other physical objects; I felt all of my emotions and desires in it and because of it; and I was aware of pains and pleasant feelings in it but in nothing else. I didn't know why sadness goes with the sensation of pain or why joy goes with sensory stimulation. I didn't know why the stomach twitchings that I call hunger warn me that I need to eat or why dryness in my throat warns me that I need to drink. Seeing no connection between stomach twitchings and the desire to eat or between the sensation of a pain-producing thing and the consequent awareness of sadness, I could only say that I had been taught the connection by nature. And nature seems also to have taught me everything else that I knew about the objects of sensation—for I convinced myself that the sensations came to me in a certain way before having found grounds on which to prove that they did.

But, since then, many experiences have shaken my faith in the senses. Towers that seemed round from a distance sometimes looked square from close up, and huge statues on pediments sometimes didn't look big when seen from the ground. In innumerable such cases, I found the judgments of the external senses to be wrong. And the same holds for the internal senses. What is felt more inwardly than pain? Yet I had heard that people with amputated arms and legs sometimes seem to feel pain in the missing limb, and it therefore didn't seem perfectly certain to me that the limb in which I feel a pain is always the one that hurts. And, to these grounds for doubt, I've recently added two that are very general: First, since I didn't believe myself to sense anything while awake that I couldn't also take myself to sense in a dream, and since I didn't believe that what I sense in sleep comes from objects outside me, I didn't see why I should believe what I sense while awake comes from such objects. Second, since I didn't yet know my creator (or, rather, since I supposed that I didn't know Him), I saw nothing to rule out my having been so designed by nature that I'm deceived even in what seems most obviously true to me.

And I could easily refute the reasoning by which I convinced myself of the reality of sensible things. Since my nature seemed to impel me toward many things that my reason rejected, I didn't believe that I ought to have much faith in nature's teachings. And, while my will didn't control my sense perceptions, I didn't believe it to follow that these perceptions came from outside me, since I thought that the ability to produce these ideas might be in me without my being aware of it.

Now that I've begun to know myself and my creator better, I still believe that I oughtn't blindly to accept everything that I seem to get from the senses. Yet I no longer believe that I ought to call it all into doubt.

In the first place, I know that everything that I clearly and distinctly understand can be made by God to be exactly as I understand it. The fact that I can clearly and distinctly understand one thing apart from another is therefore enough to make me certain that it is distinct from the other, since the things could be separated by God if not by something else. (I judge the things to be distinct regardless of the power needed to make them exist separately.) Accordingly, from the fact that I have gained knowledge of my existence without noticing anything about my nature or essence except that I am a thinking thing, I can rightly conclude that my essence consists solely in the fact that I am a thinking thing. It's possible (or, as I will say later, it's certain) that I have a body which is very tightly bound to me. But, on the one hand, I have a clear and distinct idea of myself insofar as I am just a thinking and unextended thing, and, on the other hand, I have a distinct idea of my body insofar as it is just an extended and unthinking thing. It's certain, then, that I am really distinct from my body and can exist without it.

In addition, I find in myself abilities for special modes of awareness, like the abilities to have mental images and to sense. I can clearly and distinctly conceive of my whole self as something that lacks these abilities, but I can't conceive of the abilities' existing without me, or without an understanding substance in which to reside. Since the conception of these abilities includes the conception of something that understands, I see that these abilities are distinct from me in the way that a thing's properties are distinct from the thing itself.

I recognize other abilities in me, like the ability to move around and to assume various postures. These abilities can't be understood to exist apart from a substance in which they reside any more than the abilities to imagine and sense, and they therefore cannot exist without such a substance. But it's obvious that, if these abilities do exist, the substance in which they reside must be a body or extended substance rather than an understanding one—for the clear and distinct conceptions of these abilities contain extension but not understanding.

There is also in me, however, a passive ability to sense—to receive and recognize ideas of sensible things. But, I wouldn't be able to put this ability to use if there weren't, either in me or in something else, an active power to produce or make sensory ideas. Since this active power doesn't presuppose understanding, and since it often produces ideas in me without my cooperation and even against my will, it cannot exist in me. Therefore, this power must exist in a substance distinct from me. And, for reasons that I've noted, this substance must contain, either formally or eminently, all the reality that is contained subjectively in the ideas that the power produces. Either this substance is a physical object (a thing of bodily nature that contains formally the reality that the idea contains subjectively), or it is God or one of His creations that is higher than a physical object (something that contains this reality eminently). But, since God isn't a deceiver, it's completely obvious that He doesn't send these ideas to me directly or by means of a creation that contains their reality eminently rather than formally. For, since He has not given me any ability to recognize that these ideas are sent by Him or by creations other than physical objects, and since He has given me a strong inclination to believe that the ideas come from physical objects, I see no way to avoid the conclusion that He deceives me if the ideas are sent to me by anything other than physical objects. It follows that physical objects exist. These objects may not exist exactly as I comprehend them by sense; in many ways, sensory comprehension is obscure and confused. But these objects must at least have in them everything that I clearly and distinctly understand them to have—every general property within the scope of pure mathematics.

But what about particular properties, such as the size and shape of the sun? And what about things that I understand less clearly than mathematical properties, like light, sound, and pain? These are open to doubt. But, since God isn't a deceiver, and since I therefore have the God-given ability to correct any falsity that may be in my beliefs, I have high hopes of finding the truth about even these things. There is undoubtedly some truth in everything I have been taught by nature—for, when I use the term "nature" in its general sense, I refer to God Himself or to the order that He has established in the created world, and, when I apply the term specifically to *my* nature, I refer to the collection of everything that God has given *me.*

Nature teaches me nothing more explicitly, however, than that I have a body which is hurt when I feel pain, which needs food or drink when I experience hunger or thirst, and so on. Accordingly, I ought not to doubt that there is some truth to this.

Through sensations like pain, hunger, and thirst, nature also teaches me that I am not present in my body in the way that a sailor is present in his ship. Rather, I am very tightly bound to my body and so "mixed up" with it that we form a single thing. If this weren't so, I—who am just a thinking thing—wouldn't feel pain when my body was injured; I would perceive the injury by pure understanding in the way that a sailor sees the leaks in his ship with his eyes. And, when my body needed food or drink, I would explicitly understand that the need existed without having the confused sensations of hunger and thirst. For the sensations of thirst, hunger, and pain are just confused modifications of thought arising from the union and "mixture" of mind and body.

Also, nature teaches me that there are other physical objects around my body—some that I ought to seek and others that I ought to avoid. From the fact that I sense things like colors, sounds, odors, flavors, temperatures, and hardnesses, I correctly infer that sense perceptions come from physical objects that vary as widely (though perhaps not in the same way) as the perceptions do. And, from the fact that some of these perceptions are pleasant while others are unpleasant, I infer with certainty that my body—or, rather, my whole self which consists of a body and a mind—can be benefited and harmed by the physical objects around it.

There are many other things that I seem to have been taught by nature but that I have really accepted out of a habit of thoughtless judgment. These things may well be false. Among them are the judgments that a space is empty if nothing in it happens to affect my senses; that a hot physical object has something in it resembling my idea of heat; that a white or green thing has in it the same whiteness or greenness that I sense; that a bitter or sweet thing has in it the same flavor that I taste; that stars, towers, and other physical objects have the same size and shape that they present to my senses; and so on.

If I am to avoid accepting what is indistinct in these cases, I must more carefully explain my use of the phrase "taught by nature." In particular, I should say that I am now using the term "nature" in a narrower sense than when I took it to refer to the whole complex of what God has given me. This complex includes much having to do with my mind alone (such as my grasp of the fact that what is done cannot be undone and the rest of what I know by the light of nature) which does not bear on what I am now saying. And the complex also includes much having to do with my body alone (such as its tendency to go downward) with which I am not dealing now. I'm now using the term "nature" to refer only to what God has given me insofar as I am a composite of mind and body. It is this nature that teaches me to avoid that which occasions painful sensations, to seek that which occasions pleasant sensations, and so on. But this nature seems not to teach me to draw conclusions about external objects from sense perceptions without first having examined the matter with my understanding—for true knowledge of external things seems to belong to the mind alone, not to the composite of mind and body.

Thus, while a star has no more effect on my eye than a flame, this does not really produce a positive inclination to believe that the star is as small as the flame; for my youthful judgment about the size of the flame, I had no real grounds. And, while I feel heat when I approach a fire and pain when I draw nearer, I have absolutely no reason for believing that something in the fire resembles the heat, just as I have no reason for believing that something in the fire resembles the pain; I only have reason for believing that there is something or other in the fire that produces the feelings of heat and pain. And, although there may be nothing in a given region of space that affects my senses, it doesn't follow that there aren't any physical objects in that space. Rather I now see that, on these matters and others, I used to pervert the natural order of things. For, while nature has given sense perceptions to my mind for the sole purpose of indicating what is beneficial and what harmful to the composite of which my mind is a part, and while the perceptions are sufficiently clear and distinct for that purpose, I used these perceptions as standards for identifying the essence of physical objects—an essence which they only reveal obscurely and confusedly.

I've already explained how it can be that, despite God's goodness, my judgments can be false. But a new difficulty arises here—one having to do with the things that nature presents to me as desirable or undesirable and also with the errors that I seem to have found in my internal sensations. One of these errors seems to be committed, for example, when a man is fooled by some food's pleasant taste into eating poison hidden in that food. But surely, in this case, what the man's nature impels him to eat is the good tasting food, not the poison of which he knows nothing. We can draw no conclusion except that his nature isn't omniscient, and this conclusion isn't surprising. Since a man is a limited thing, he can only have limited perfections.

Still, we often err in cases in which nature does impel us. This happens, for example, when sick people want food or drink that would quickly harm them. To say that these people err as a result of the corruption of their nature does not solve the problem—for a sick man is no less a creation of God than a well one, and it seems as absurd to suppose that God has given him a deceptive nature. A clock made of wheels and weights follows the natural laws just as precisely when it is poorly made and inaccurate as when it does everything that its maker wants. Thus, if I regard a human body as a machine made up of bones, nerves, muscles, veins, blood, and skin such that even without a mind it would do just what it does now (except for things that require a mind because they are controlled by the will), it's easy to see that what happens to a sick man is no less "natural" than what happens to a well one. For instance, if a body suffers from dropsy, it has a dry throat of the sort that regularly brings the sensation of thirst to the mind, the dryness disposes the nerves and other organs to drink, and the drinking makes the illness worse. But this is just as natural as when a similar dryness of throat moves a person who is perfectly healthy to take a drink that is beneficial. Bearing in mind my conception of a clock's use, I might say that an inaccurate clock departs from its nature, and, similarly, viewing the machine of the human body as designed for its usual motions, I can say that it drifts away from its nature if it has a dry throat when drinking will not help to maintain it. I should note, however, that the sense in which I am now using the term "nature" differs from that in which I used it before. For, as I have just used the term "nature," the nature of a man (or clock) is something that depends on my thinking of the difference between a sick and a well man (or of the difference between a poorly made and a well-made clock)—something regarded as extrinsic to the things. But, when I used "nature" before, I referred to something which is *in* things and which therefore has some reality.

It may be that we just offer an extrinsic description of a body suffering from dropsy when, noting that it has a dry throat but doesn't need to drink, we say that its nature is corrupted. Still, the description is not purely extrinsic when we say that a composite or union of mind and body has a corrupted nature. There is a real fault in the composite's nature, for it is thirsty when drinking would be harmful. It therefore remains to be asked why God's goodness doesn't prevent *this* nature's being deceptive.

To begin the answer, I'll note that mind differs importantly from body in that body is by its nature divisible while mind is indivisible. When I think about my mind—or, in other words, about myself insofar as I am just a thinking thing—I can't distinguish any parts in me; I understand myself to be a single, unified thing. Although my whole mind seems united to my whole body, I know that cutting off a foot, arm, or other limb would not take anything away from my mind. The abilities to will, sense, understand, and so on can't be called parts, since it's one and the same mind that wills, senses, and understands. On the other hand, whenever I think of a physical or extended thing, I can mentally divide it, and I therefore understand that the object is divisible. This single fact would be enough to teach me that my mind and body are distinct, if I hadn't already learned that in another way.

Next, I notice that the mind isn't directly affected by all parts of the body, but only by the brain—or maybe just by the small part of the brain containing the so-called "common sense." Whenever this part of the brain is in a given state, it presents the same thing to the mind, regardless of what is happening in the rest of the body (as is shown by innumerable experiments that I need not review here).

In addition, I notice that the nature of body is such that, if a first part can be moved by a second that is far away, the first part can be moved in exactly the same way by something between the first and second without the second part's being affected. For example, if A, B, C, and D are points on a cord, and if the first point (A) can be moved in a certain way by a pull on the last point (D), then A can be moved in the same way by a pull on one of the middle points (B or C) without D's being moved. Similarly, science teaches me that, when my foot hurts, the sensation of pain is produced by nerves distributed throughout the foot which extend like cords from there to the brain. When pulled in the foot, these nerves pull the central parts of the brain to which they are attached, moving those parts in ways designated by nature to present the mind with the sensation of a pain "in the foot." But, since these nerves pass through the shins, thighs, hips, back, and neck on their way from foot to brain, it can happen that their being touched in the middle, rather than at the end in the foot, produces the same motion in the brain as when the foot is hurt and, hence, that the mind feels the same pain "in the foot." And the point holds for other sensations as well.

Finally, I notice that, since only one sensation can be produced by a given motion of the part of the brain that directly affects the mind, the best conceivable sensation for it to produce is the one that is most often useful for the maintenance of the healthy man. Experience teaches that all the sensations put in us by nature are of this sort and therefore that everything in our sensations testifies to God's power and goodness. For example, when the nerves in the foot are moved with unusual violence, the motion is communicated through the middle of the spine to the center of the brain, where it signals the mind to sense a pain "in the foot." This urges the mind to view the pain's cause as harmful to the foot and to do what it can to remove that cause. Of course, God could have so designed man's nature that the same motion of the brain presented something else to the mind, like the motion in the brain, or the motion in the foot, or a motion somewhere between the brain and foot. But no alternative to the way things are would be as conducive to the maintenance of the body. Similarly, when we need drink, the throat becomes dry, the dryness moves the nerves of the throat thereby moving the center of the brain, and the brain's movements cause the sensation of thirst in the mind. It's the sensation of thirst that is produced, because no information about our condition is more useful to us than that we need to get something to drink in order to remain healthy. And the same is true in other cases.

This makes it completely obvious that, despite God's immense goodness, the nature of man (whom we now view as a composite of mind and body) cannot fail to be deceptive. For, if something produces the movement usually associated with an injured foot in the nerve running from foot to brain or in the brain itself rather than in the foot, a pain is felt as if "in the foot." Here the senses are deceived by their nature. Since this motion in the brain must always bring the same sensation to mind, and since the motion's cause is something hurting the foot more often than something elsewhere, it's in accordance with reason that the motion always presents the mind a pain in the foot rather than elsewhere. And, if dryness of the throat arises, not (as usual) from drink's being conducive to the body's health, but (as happens in dropsy) from some other cause, it's much better that we are deceived on this occasion than that we are generally deceived when our bodies are sound. And the same holds for other cases.

In addition to helping me to be aware of the errors to which my nature is subject, these reflections help me readily to correct or avoid those errors. I know that sensory indications of what is good for my body are more often true than false; I can almost always examine a given thing with several senses; and I can also use my memory (which connects the present to the past) and my understanding (which has now examined all the causes of error). Hence, I need no longer fear that what the senses daily show me is unreal. I should reject the exaggerated doubts of the past few days as ridiculous. This is especially true of the chief ground for these doubts—namely, my inability to distinguish dreaming from being awake. For I now notice that dreaming and being awake are importantly different: the events in dreams are not linked by memory to the rest of my life like those that happen while I am awake. If, while I'm awake, someone were suddenly to appear and then immediately to disappear without my seeing where he came from or went to (as happens in dreams), I would justifiably judge that he was not a real man but a ghost—or, better, an apparition created in my brain. But, if I distinctly observe something's source, its place, and the time at which I learn about it, and if I grasp an unbroken connection between it and the rest of my life, I'm quite sure that it is something in my waking life rather than in a dream. And I ought not to have the slightest doubt about the reality of such things if I have examined them with all my senses, my memory, and my understanding without finding any conflicting evidence. For, from the fact that God is not a deceiver, it follows that I am not deceived in any case of this sort. Since the need to act does not always allow time for such a careful examination, however, we must admit the likelihood of men's erring about particular things and acknowledge the weakness of our nature.

THINKING ABOUT MEDITATION VI

You know what to do.

The major points Descartes covered were _____

_____

_____

_____ .

Some important concepts Descartes has thus far established are

1. His own existence, because every time he doubts that existence he proves that he exists. He must exist in order to doubt he exists.

2. A rule for telling true ideas from false ideas: Ideas he can conceive of clearly and distinctly are true.

3. The cause of error: His will can choose things that his understanding does not completely grasp.

4. The existence of God: God exists as the only possible source of the idea of God; an imperfect being like Descartes could not create the idea of a perfect being; that would be a case of the greater coming from the lesser, which is the same as saying the effect exceeds the cause. A second proof of God's existence is based on the idea that God must exist as the continuous re-creator of Descartes' existence. A third proof of God's existence is that His essence is tied inextricably to His existence. God is perfect, and conceiving of a perfect being who did not exist is not possible; however, a being who had all perfections but who lacked the perfection of existence would be a contradiction in terms, like the color white-black.

Note that Descartes has not yet proved he has a body! Or that the material world exists. Proving either one, of course, would provide strong evidence for the other. He begins *Meditation VI* by saying, "It remains for me to examine whether material objects exist." Let's stop here for a moment. Let us say you are like most of my students and take it as "obvious" that material objects and the material world exist. It is also obvious for me, when I am not thinking philosophically, that the material world exists. You and I, in our lives outside philosophy, are not troubled that occasionally our senses deceive us or that frequently we are in a dream world and think it is a real world. You would probably agree that your perception of the material world is occasionally wrong, but would add, so what!

Maybe an issue closer to home will help you understand Descartes' problem and his passion for finding unshakable truths about reality. Let us say you have had a friend since childhood. You have trusted this friend entirely and told your friend all your deepest secrets. You never knew your friend to lie to you or deceive you. A thousand times, your friend has proved reliable. Then one day, on an important issue, your friend deceives you deliberately and completely. Could you ever again have the same complete faith and trust in your friend as you had before this deceit?

I would honestly say _____

_____ .

Personally I would try to forgive the friend, but the relationship would never be the same. I might trust my friend eventually, but I would never naively trust my friend again. Descartes is in a similar but worse situation. The truth you and I hunger for in personal relationships he hungers for about the world. He believes many things about the material world and is wrong every time his senses deceive him or he dreams. Deception breaks the precious unity between yourself and your friend. Error breaks the precious unity between the philosopher and reality. Friends hunger for the bonds produced by love. The philosopher hungers for the bonds produced by understanding. In the *Meditations on First Philosophy,* we see Descartes seeking the truths that will hold his world together.

By the beginning of *Meditation VI,* Descartes knows God exists. He says toward the middle of the Meditation that "God isn't a deceiver." Therefore, Descartes can be certain that the material world exists, because God has given him a "strong inclination" to believe it exists. Descartes is taught "by nature" to believe that the material world exists. In other words, it is so effortlessly automatic for him to believe that the material world exists that it must be part of his nature to believe so. Since God created Descartes' nature, the material world must exist or God would be a deceiver. But Descartes is not completely satisfied. Sometimes people seem to be taught "by nature" to do things that are harmful to themselves. Then is God a deceiver after all, since He is the author of our "nature"?

"[1] . . . we often err in cases in which nature does impel us. This happens, for example, when sick people want food or drink that would quickly harm them. [2] To say that these people err as a result of the corruption of their nature does not solve the problem—for a sick man is no less a creation of God than a well one, and it seems as absurd to suppose that God has given him a deceptive nature."

In other words?

In other words, in 1 he says _____

_____ . An example of my own would be

_____ .

In 2 he argues _____

_____ .

Thus the problem remains. Why are we led "by nature" to do things that are harmful? This really asks, how can God be perfect and make an imperfect being?

Previously, Descartes has answered problems about simpler cases of error. If my senses tell me that I see a round tower in the distance, I should wait until I have enough information to judge whether the tower is really round. God is not responsible for my error because there is nothing in my nature that forces me "naturally" to say square towers are round. But what if I am ill and my throat is parched and drinking water is exactly what will make me sicker? I seem to be led by my very nature to do something that would also be destructive. Isn't God to blame at this point for making my nature so imperfect that it is self-harming?

Doesn't Descartes argue against this very point by saying _____

_____

_____ ?

Here are the two passages you may be thinking about.

". . . when we need drink, the throat becomes dry, the dryness moves the nerves of the throat thereby moving the center of the brain, and the brain's movements cause the sensation of thirst in the mind. It's the sensation of thirst that is produced, because no information about our condition is more useful to us than that we need to get something to drink in order to remain healthy." ". . . if dryness of the throat arises, not (as usual) from drink's being conducive to the body's health, but (as happens in dropsy) from some other cause, it's much better that we are deceived on this occasion than that we are generally deceived when our bodies are sound."

One more time. In other words?

He is saying that it is better if _____

_____ because _____

_____ .

It would be worse if _____

_____ because _____

_____ .

Now, near the end of *Meditation VI*, he gives his answer to the problem of dreams. Remember, the problem was that there seems to be no way of telling dreams from waking. I proposed a test for you to tell the difference between the two. Can you find the passage where Descartes tries to pass the same test?

It is in the last long paragraph where he says, " _____

_____

_____

_____ ."

In essence, he is saying _____

_____

_____ . When I compare what he said with

what Descartes said in *Meditation I*, I see _____

_____

_____ .

If you could learn only one thing from Descartes, what would it be?

The most important lesson Descartes has to teach me is _____

_____

_____ .

Remember that.

Exercise 6.1

Check the questions below that Descartes answers in *Meditation VI*, and then number them in the order in which they occur.

a. How can we tell dreaming from waking?

b. Can we be certain of the existence of physical objects?

c. Is God to blame for errors our God-given nature impels us to commit?

d. What is the origin of dreams?

e. What is the difference between mental images and our understanding?

f. What is the nature of sin?

Exercise 6.2

Arrange the following concepts in the order in which they occur in *Meditation VI*.

a. If we were constructed so that we could avoid the few errors our nature impels us toward when we are sick, we would err more often when we are healthy.

b. Descartes reviews his major beliefs before the *Meditations*.

c. A "motion" in the body can affect the brain (and thus the mind) in only one way.

d. Descartes reviews the reasons he has learned during the *Meditations* for doubting his beliefs.

e. The mind, a thinking thing of no size, is absolutely distinct from the body, a nonthinking thing with a size. [This is stated several places; find the first place.]

f. Dreaming can be distinguished from waking.

g. Descartes can be certain that physical objects have, at least, the mathematical properties he clearly and distinctly understands them to have.

h. Because mental images are distinct from, and not necessarily produced by, the understanding, they might be copies of physical objects.

i. Descartes describes a method for destroying doubts (aroused in *Meditation I*) about what his senses tell him.

Exercise 6.3

Read the following paragraph carefully.

"[1] I recognize other abilities in me, like the ability to move around and to assume various postures. [2] These abilities can't be understood to exist apart from a substance in which they reside any more than the abilities to imagine and sense, and they therefore cannot exist without such a substance. [3] But it's obvious that, if these abilities do exist, the substance in which they reside must be a body or extended substance rather than an understanding one—for the clear and distinct conceptions of these abilities contain extension but not understanding."

1. Descartes is attempting to prove the existence of
    a. A substance his abilities reside in
    b. Abilities
    c. Substances
    d. Substances the mind resides in
    e. His mind

2. Descartes reasons from
    a. The existence of abilities to the existence of his senses
    b. The existence of his senses to the existence of abilities
    c. The existence of a substance to the existence of abilities the substance resides in
    d. The existence of his abilities to the existence of a substance the abilities reside in

3. Descartes is establishing these points to eventually show that
    a. The mind exists
    b. The body exists
    c. Abilities exist
    d. God exists
    e. God exists as the creator of Descartes' body

Exercise 6.4

Read the following paragraph carefully.

"For, since He has not given me any ability to recognize that these ideas are sent by Him or by creations other than physical objects, and since He has given me a strong inclination to believe that the ideas come from physical objects, I see no way to avoid the conclusion that He deceives me if the ideas are sent to me by anything other than physical objects."

1. Check each of the following statements that could be correctly inferred from this passage.
    a. "These ideas" refers to ideas that come from physical objects.
    b. Physical objects exist because they come from God.
    c. God is a deceiver.
    d. God is not a deceiver.

e. Physical objects exist because they produce ideas that God has given Descartes a strong inclination to believe come from physical objects.

f. Ideas exist because they produce conceptions of God-created physical objects.

Exercise 6.5

Read the following paragraph carefully.

"And, although there may be nothing in a given region of space that affects my senses, it doesn't follow that there aren't any physical objects in that space. Rather I now see that, on these matters and others, I used to pervert the natural order of things. For, while nature has given sense perceptions to my mind for the sole purpose of indicating what is beneficial and what harmful to the composite of which my mind is a part, and while the perceptions are sufficiently clear and distinct for that purpose, I used these perceptions as standards for identifying the essence of physical objects—an essence which they only reveal obscurely and confusedly."

1. Place a check beside statements that are consistent with the above.
   a. Nothing exists in space.
   b. The purpose of sense perceptions is to identify the essence of physical objects.
   c. The purpose of sense perceptions is to help us find what is good for us and avoid what is harmful.
   d. Sense perceptions are not accurate enough to help us find what is good for us and avoid what is harmful.
   e. We make a serious mistake when we assume sense perceptions, which are suitable for helping us find what is good and avoiding what is harmful, clearly and distinctly tell us the essence of physical objects.

Exercise 6.6: Review

You are now ready to review some major features of Descartes' argument in the *Meditations*. Arrange the following concepts in the order in which they occur in *Meditations I–VI*. Pick any two and decide which comes first. Then add another concept and decide where it goes, and so forth. As your ordered list grows longer, you may have to consult the *Meditations*.

a. Physical objects, at least as mathematical entities, exist.
b. There must be as much reality in an effect as in a cause.
c. Descartes is a thinking thing.
d. Descartes has an idea of God.
e. Anything known clearly and distinctly must be true.
f. Descartes exists.
g. Because God's existence cannot be divided from His essence, God exists.

h. The will is unlimited and the understanding is limited.
i. God is the cause of Descartes' idea of God.
j. God exists as the continued cause of Descartes' existence.
k. Error is caused when the will's judgment exceeds the understanding's clear and distinct knowledge.
l. Descartes' parents are not the cause of his continued existence.
m. God is no deceiver.
n. Dreams can be told from waking.
o. Dreams cannot be told from waking.
p. Descartes imagines an evil demon who is continuously fooling him.
q. Knowledge of God's existence is innate.

AN ANALYSIS OF YOUR PHILOSOPHICAL SELF-PORTRAIT

To see how your views from page 11 stack up against Descartes', read my analysis below, rethink your position, and then circle what you believe is the correct answer. I've underlined Descartes' answers.

1. T F *Very little, if anything, can be known for certain.*

   As you saw in *Meditation I*, Descartes *begins* by doubting everything. However, by the end of *Meditation VI*, he has established a long list of certitudes. If you are a skeptic, then prepare to meet one of your toughest opponents. If you believe skeptics are wrong, then Descartes may be one of your strongest allies.

2. T F *From the fact that you are a thinking being, it is possible to prove that you exist.*

   This concept is at the core of Descartes' philosophy. Even if I can't tell whether I'm awake or asleep or whether the physical universe exists or whether God exists or even whether $2 + 2 = 4$, I can certainly know that I am *thinking* about these things. Thus, I can be sure that I am a thinking being. And if I know I am a thinking being, I certainly also know that I exist. How could I be a thinking being, if I, the one doing the thinking, *didn't* exist? Thus, it seems obviously true that from the fact that I am a thinking being, I can prove that I exist.

   Many philosophers, however, argue that Descartes is wrong.
   What error do you see in his reasoning?

   Perhaps his error is _____

   _____

   _____ .

3. T F *From the fact that you exist, it is possible to prove that you are a thinking being.*

   I don't think Descartes would agree.
   Assume you know that you exist. That's all you know. If all you know is that you exist, you could not prove that you are a thinking

being. You can't get from you-as-existing to you-as-thinking. In fact, whenever you start pondering the relationship between your thinking and your existence, the first truth you come up with, according to Descartes, is that you are *thinking*. Thus, the certainty of thinking comes before the certainty of existence.

4. T F *It is possible, without using knowledge gained by the senses, to prove that God exists.*

Descartes believes this is true, but many of my students, even those who believe in God, argue that it is false. They believe that one must, at least, *hear* about the concept of God, in order to know that God exists. Thus, knowledge of God comes through the senses (in this case, the ear).

Descartes would argue that no teacher could instruct you in the nature of an all-knowing, all-good, all-powerful being, because nothing remotely resembling such a being could be presented to you. Almost anything *but* God could be explained in words, but words fall infinitely short of God's divine nature. Thus, the only way you can genuinely understand the term *God* is if God Himself planted this understanding in your mind.

Do you agree or disagree?

I (agree, disagree) because _____

_____

_____ .

5. T F *You could not have the idea of a perfect being (God) unless an actual perfect being (God) existed.*

Descartes believes both that all our ideas must have some source and that we all have an idea of a perfect being. Where could this idea have come from? It could not have come from an imperfect being. How could something imperfect give us any conception of something perfect? Therefore, our idea of a perfect being could only have come from an *actual* perfect being. Therefore, God, the perfect being exists. Descartes will elaborate this important proof in *Meditation III*.

How strong, at this point, do you think the proof is?

I believe the proof is (very strong, strong, weak, very weak) because

_____

_____ .

Evaluation: Number of points in agreement with Descartes = _____ of 5 possible.

A position of Descartes' that you strongly (support, oppose) is _____

_____

because _____

_____ .

WRITING ABOUT
DESCARTES

Let's go step-by-step through preparations to write a short essay on Descartes' *Meditations on First Philosophy*. The assignment is to summarize Descartes' arguments in *Meditation I* and then select one for critical analysis. To begin, all you have to do is fill in the following blanks.

The body of the paper will obviously be divided into _____ parts.

In the first part of the body, I will summarize _____

_____ . In the remaining part of the body, I

will criticize his argument that _____ .

The next thing to do is go back and look at *Meditation I*. Draw a line across the page wherever Descartes seems to begin a new argument. Look at your margin notes and underlinings. Reread our discussion after *Meditation I*, and make a list of things you want to be sure to cover in summarizing his arguments.

I will want to talk about all of the following: _____

_____

_____

_____ .

Look at this list and decide which of Descartes' arguments are the weakest. To make things simpler, we will say that to perform a "critical analysis" of an argument is to show its strengths and its weaknesses. Like a movie critic, a philosophical critic tries to see both the positive and the negative aspects of his or her subject.

The argument I want to analyze critically is _____

_____

_____ .

Believe it or not, you have just finished a rough outline. Now, let's start adding details.

Go back and find sections of *Meditation I* that you want to quote directly in either part of the body.

The page numbers are _____

_____ .

Now write one of the quotations and practice putting it into your own words and adding an original example. (This will be one major part of your work in both the summary and the criticism.)

Descartes says, " _____

_____

_____ ." This means _____

_____

_____ . An example of this would be

_____ .

Practice that one more time.

In another place, Descartes says, " _____

_____

_____ ." His point is

_____

_____ . A clear example of this would be

_____ .

Use these three techniques in the body of your summary: Quote what he says, explain it in your own words, and think of examples or additional ways of explaining his meaning. When in doubt, add more. In thirty years of teaching, I have never written "too much explanation" in the margin of a student's paper.

Now let's think in more detail about the argument you want to criticize. You will have already summarized its major features in the first part of your paper. It would be a good idea to begin the critical analysis by restating the argument, as we have done occasionally on this tour, as a list of sentences, using one sentence for each important point. Select one argument from *Meditation I* and state its first three major ideas.

I will select Descartes' argument about _____

_____ . I believe this argument involves _____

steps. The first major point is _____

_____ .

The second point is _____

_____ .

The third point is _____

_____ .

    Once you have restated the argument (and perhaps expanded any unclear points with original examples), you will be ready to evaluate its strengths and its weaknesses. You have had some practice in this already on the tour. Think about each aspect of Descartes' argument. Try to see the world as he does. What could you add to some points to make them clearer, stronger, more relevant? What ideas in the argument seem weak? Think of strong counterarguments. What are the obvious facts, observations, or principles that back up your view and show the weaknesses of Descartes' view? Try to find several ways of explaining your point.

    Select one of the weakest assertions in the argument you just stated and practice criticizing its flaws.

One of the weakest parts of Descartes' argument is his statement

that " _____

_____

_____ ."

The point he is trying to make is _____

_____ .

An example of this would be _____

_____ .

In essence, I believe he is wrong because _____

_____ .

My reasons for saying this are _____

_____

_____ .

For example, _____

_____ .

Another way of putting my criticism would be _____

_____

_____ [and so forth

as you expand your analysis of a weakness in the argument].

    Thus far, you have created a rough outline, isolated key sections of Descartes' *Meditation I,* and found some simple techniques for summarizing and criticizing arguments. Now let's talk for a moment about transitions. A transition sentence is often useful at the end of a paragraph, especially when the next paragraph begins a new topic.

Here is a sample transition sentence: "After finishing his summary of his argument about the senses, Descartes moves on to a proof of God's existence."

If the previous sentence came at the end of a paragraph, you would

assume that the paragraph had been about _____ .
You would also assume that the next paragraph would be about

_____ .

The simplest way to write transition sentences is to make sure they have two parts. The first part refers to the previous paragraph. The second part refers to the next paragraph. Use this same two-part construction at key places in your Descartes essay.

Now let's think about introductions and conclusions. Keep your introductions short. Here is a sample:

There are _____ [insert a number] main arguments in *Meditation I.* [Now add one sentence for each main argument.] The first

argument involves _____

_____ .

The essential idea in the second argument is _____

_____ [and so forth, until you are ready to talk about the arguments you will

strengthen]. The argument I will criticize is _____

_____ .

In a short essay of under five pages, the conclusion does not have to do much more than summarize your main points. Often you can simply state, in a more general way, the ideas in your introduction.

Now that we are almost finished, here are a few last random pieces of advice about writing college papers.

- ❖ The more work you do before you start writing, the less work writing will be.
- ❖ Learn to use a word processing program.
- ❖ Talk about your paper with a fellow student.
- ❖ Seek extra help from your teacher.
- ❖ Divide the job into as many small tasks as possible, and spread them out over as many days as possible. Better to spend five hours on five separate days than to spend five miserable hours between midnight and dawn.
- ❖ Don't try to finish in fewer than three drafts.
- ❖ Stock up on good things to eat before you start.

APPENDIX A

Selections from Anselm, Aquinas, and Augustine

A SELF-TEST

Each of the following three selections bears an important relationship to Descartes' *Meditations on First Philosophy.* Two of the three (Anselm's and Aquinas') present proofs for God's existence. Read each carefully, underline important points, and paraphrase key ideas in the margin. Each proof, taken as a whole, provides either a strong philosophical similarity or a strong philosophical contrast to Descartes' proofs of God's existence. Label ideas that are clearly similar to Descartes' approach with an *S*; label ideas that are clearly different from Descartes' approach with a *D*.

The selection from Augustine's *Confessions* contains the first formulation of a key concept from Descartes' *Meditations.* Find this passage in Augustine and explain its link to Descartes with a margin note.

ST. ANSELM'S ONTOLOGICAL ARGUMENT

This selection is excerpted from Anselm's **Proslogium** *translated by Ronald Rubin (Claremont: Areté Press, 1984).*

Chapter II, God Truly Exists So Lord—you who reward faith with understanding—let me understand, insofar as you see fit, whether you are as we believe and whether you are what we believe you to be. We believe you to be something than which nothing greater can be conceived. The question, then, is whether something with this nature exists, since "the fool has said in his heart that there is no God" [Ps. 14:1, 53:1]. But, surely, when the fool hears the words "something than which nothing greater can be conceived," he understands what he hears, and what he understands exists in his understanding—even if he doesn't think that it exists. For it is one thing for an object to exist in someone's understanding, and another for him to think that it exists. When a painter plans out a painting, he has it in his understanding, but—not yet having produced it—he doesn't yet think that it exists. After he has painted it, however, he has the painting in his understanding, and—having produced it—he thinks that it exists. Even the fool must admit, then, that something than which nothing greater can be conceived exists in the understanding—since he understands the phrase "that than which nothing greater can be conceived" when he hears it, and whatever he understands exists in his understanding. And surely that than which a greater cannot be conceived cannot exist *just* in the understanding. If it were to exist *just* in the understanding, we could conceive of its existing in reality too, in which case it would be greater. Therefore, if that than which a greater cannot be conceived exists just in the understanding, the very thing than which a greater *cannot* be conceived is something than which a greater *can* be conceived. But clearly this cannot be. Without doubt, then, something than which a greater can't be conceived does exist—both in the understanding and in reality.

Chapter III, It Is Impossible to Think That God Doesn't Exist   In fact, this thing so truly exists that it can't be thought not to exist. For a thing that can be conceived to exist but can't be conceived not to exist is greater than one that can be conceived not to exist. Hence, if that than which a greater can't be conceived could be conceived not to exist, that than which a greater can't be conceived would not be that than which a greater can't be conceived. But this would be a contradiction. Therefore, something than which a greater can't be conceived so truly exists that it can't be thought not to exist.

And this thing is you, Lord our God. Therefore, you so truly exist, Lord my God, that you can't be thought not to exist. And this is as it should be. For, if one's mind could conceive of something better than you, a created thing would rise above its creator and pass judgment on him, which would be completely absurd. Indeed, anything other than you can be thought not to exist. Therefore, you alone have the truest, and hence the greatest, being of all; nothing else has being as true or great. Then why has the fool said in his heart that there is no God, when it is evident to a rational mind that your being is the greatest of all? Why—unless because he was stupid and a fool!

AQUINAS' FIVE WAYS

This selection is from Aquinas' **Summa Theologica,** *Part One, Question 2, article 3. The translation is by Ronald Rubin.*

There are five ways to prove that God exists.

The first and clearest way derives from facts about change. Clearly, as our senses show, some things in the world do change. But everything that changes is made to change by something else. A thing undergoes a change only insofar as it has a potentiality for being that into which it changes. But a thing causes change only insofar as it is actual; to cause change is just to draw something out of potentiality into actuality, which can only be done by something that is in actuality. (Thus, something actually hot, like fire, makes wood that is potentially hot become actually hot, thereby changing and altering that wood.) But, while a single thing can simultaneously be in actuality with respect to one property and in potentiality with respect to another, it cannot simultaneously be in actuality and potentiality with respect to one and the same property. (While that which is actually hot may simultaneously be potentially cold, that which is actually hot cannot simultaneously be potentially hot.) It is therefore impossible for a thing that undergoes a change to cause that change, or for something to change itself. Therefore, whatever undergoes change must be changed by another thing. And, if this other thing undergoes change, it also must be changed by something else, and so on. But this cannot go back to infinity; if it did, there would be no first cause of change and, consequently, no other causes of change—for something can be a secondary cause of change only if it is changed by a primary cause (as a stick moves something only if a hand moves the stick). We must therefore posit a first cause of change, that is not itself changed by anything, and this everyone understands to be God.

The second way derives from the nature of efficient causation. In the world that we sense, we find that efficient causes come in series. We do not, and cannot, find that something is its own efficient cause—for, if something were its own efficient cause, it would be prior to itself, which is impossible. But the series of efficient causes cannot possibly go back to infinity. In all series of causes, a first thing causes one or more intermediaries, and the intermediaries cause the last thing; when a cause is taken out of this series, so is its effect. Hence, if there were no first efficient cause, there would be no last or intermediate efficient causes. If the series of efficient causes went back to infinity, however, there would be no first efficient cause and thus no last or intermediate causes. But there obviously are such causes. We must therefore posit a first efficient cause, which everyone understands to be God.

The third way, which derives from facts about possibility and necessity, is this: In the world, we find some things that can either exist or fail to exist—things that are generated and corrupted and that therefore exist at some times but not others. It is impossible, however, that everything is of this sort. If something *can* fail to exist, there must have been a time at which it *has* failed to exist. Hence, if everything could fail to exist, there would have been a time at which nothing existed. But, if there had been such a time, there would not be anything in the world now—for something can begin to exist only if brought into existence by something already in existence. Therefore, if there once had been nothing in existence, it would have been impossible for anything to come into existence, and there would be nothing now. But it is obviously false that there is nothing now. Therefore, not every entity can fail to exist; there must be something in the world that exists of necessity. But, if something exists of necessity, either this necessity is or is not caused by something else. And the series of necessary beings whose necessity is caused by another cannot possibly go back to infinity. (Just as the series of efficient causes cannot go back to infinity, as we have proved.) We must therefore posit something that is necessary *per se*—something that does not owe its necessity to anything else but which causes the necessity of other things—and this everyone understands to be God.

The fourth way derives from the gradations we find in things. Some things are found to be better, truer, or nobler than others. But something is said to have more or less of a quality according to its distance from a maximum. (Thus, the hotter a thing is, the closer it is to that which is maximally hot.) Hence, there is something maximally true, good, and noble. And this thing must be the greatest being—for, as Aristotle says in *Metaphysics II* [993b25–30], those things that are greatest in truth are greatest in being. As Aristotle says in the same work [993b25], however, the greatest thing of a kind is the cause of everything of that kind (as fire, the hottest thing, is the cause of everything hot). There is therefore something that is the cause of being, goodness, and whatever other perfections there may be in things, and this we call God.

The fifth way derives from facts about the governance of the world. We see that even things lacking consciousness, such as physical objects, act for an end. They almost always act in the same way and tend toward what is best, and this shows that they achieve their ends, not by chance, but on purpose. But something that lacks consciousness can tend toward an end only if directed by something with consciousness and intelligence. (Thus, the arrow must be directed by the archer.) There is therefore some intelligence that directs everything in nature toward an end, and this we call God.

FROM THE CITY OF GOD
(BY SAINT AUGUSTINE)

This selection was taken from the T. and T. Clark edition of the Works of Aurelius Augustine, *edited by Marcus Dods, 1887.*

Book XI, Chapter 26. Of the Image of the Supreme Trinity, Which We Find in Some Sort in Human Nature Even in Its Present State And indeed we recognize in ourselves the image of God, that is, of the supreme Trinity, an image that, though it be not equal to God or rather though it be very far removed from Him—being neither coeternal nor, to say all in a word, consubstantial with Him—is yet nearer to Him in nature than any other of His works and is destined to be yet restored, that it may bear a still closer resemblance. For we both are and know that we are and delight in our being and our knowledge of it. Moreover, in these three things no true-seeing illusion disturbs us; for we do not come into contact with these by some bodily sense, as we perceive the things outside of us—colors, for example, by seeing, sounds by hearing, smells by smelling, tastes by tasting, hard and soft objects by touching— of all which sensible objects it is the images resembling them, but not themselves, that we perceive in the mind and hold in the memory and that excite us to desire the objects. But without any delusive representation of images or phantasm I am most certain that I am and that I know and delight in this. In respect of these truths I am not at all afraid of the arguments of the Academicians, who say, What if you are deceived? For if I am deceived, I am. For he who is not, cannot be deceived; and if I am deceived, by this same token I am. And since I am, how am I deceived in believing that I am? For it is certain that I am if I am deceived. Since, therefore, I, the person deceived, should exist, even if I were deceived, certainly I am not deceived in this knowledge that I am. And consequently neither am I deceived in knowing that I know. For, as I know that I am, so I know this also; that I know.

APPENDIX B

Evidence, Conclusions, and Argument Surgery

Part, if not all, of your difficulty with Descartes, is in dissecting his arguments. What is an argument and how do you dissect it?

Think of an argument as something you are trying to slice into two parts, evidence and conclusion. Evidence is one or more pieces of information that support the conclusion. The conclusion is what needs to be proved.

Here is an argument from an imaginary trial

Evidence: The print of a size 11 shoe was found in the victim's blood.

Evidence: Nelly wears a size 11 shoe.

Conclusion: Nelly is the killer.

The question in an argument is always whether the evidence will support the conclusion. Nelly wears size 11 shoes, and so did the killer. Can we conclude that Nelly did the foul deed? Not on the basis of the evidence presented. The argument establishes only one connection between Nelly and the killer. They wear the same size shoe.

Let's make the argument somewhat stronger by adding evidence that supplies a second connection between Nelly and the killer.

Evidence: The print of a size 11 shoe was found in the victim's blood.

Evidence: Nelly wears a size 11 shoe.

Evidence: Nelly was seen in the neighborhood at the time of the killing.

Conclusion: Nelly is the killer.

Note that as we add more evidence, the argument becomes somewhat stronger. Now Nelly has two connections to the killing. First, she has the shoe size of the killer, and second, she was in the area at the time of the murder. Let's add another piece of evidence.

Evidence: The print of a size 11 shoe was found in the victim's blood.

Evidence: Nelly wears a size 11 shoe.

Evidence: Nelly was seen in the neighborhood at the time of the killing.

Evidence: Nelly's diary contained a plan to murder the victim.

Conclusion: Nelly is the killer.

Things are getting tighter for Nelly. As the argument against her gets stronger, the evidence more and more supports the conclusion. Now there are three connections between Nelly and the killer: shoe size, location, and plan.

In stronger arguments, evidence captures the conclusion; in weaker arguments (like the first Nelly argument), evidence and conclusion fall apart. Your goal in dissecting an argument into evidence pieces and conclusion pieces is to tell if the argument is strong or weak.

Look at this selection from *Meditation I.*

"Since a building collapses when its foundation is cut out from under it, I will go straight to the principles on which all my former beliefs rested."

Think of evidence as a "because" statement and a conclusion as a "therefore" statement. Thus, a simple argument would have one "because" statement (one piece of evidence) supporting one "therefore" statement (one conclusion). Using this concept, you can easily carve arguments into evidence pieces and conclusion pieces by inserting "because" before what you think might be the evidence and "therefore" before what you think might be the conclusion. After making the insertions, reread the argument. If it doesn't sound right, switch the positions of "because" and "therefore."

For example, which makes more sense?

1. "[Because] a building collapses when its foundation is cut out from under it,"
   "[therefore] I will go straight to the principles on which all my former beliefs rested."

Does that make sense? We'll try switching the "because" and "therefore" (and keep the because statement first).

2. "[Because] I will go straight to the principles on which all my former beliefs rested,"
   "[therefore] a building collapses when its foundation is cut out from under it."

You can see that the first argument makes more sense than the second argument. Using the evidence of what happens to a building when its foundation is removed, Descartes moves to the conclusion that he should attack the foundational principles of his former beliefs.

When you think you have successfully carved an argument into evidence and conclusion, apply one more test. Ask yourself if the evidence is more obvious than the conclusion. Almost all arguments move from evidence that is more obvious toward a conclusion that is less obvious.

In the simple argument above, Descartes makes one statement about what happens to a building when its foundation is removed and a second statement about how he should proceed to attack the edifice of his beliefs. The behavior of a building without a foundation is more obvious than anything to do with the architectural weaknesses of belief structures. Because it is obvious what buildings do when they have no foundation, the statement about buildings must be the evidence. Thus, we have correctly dissected the argument. We have shown how Descartes reasons from evidence (the more obvious) to conclusion (the less obvious).

Now, how do you evaluate the strength of an argument? How do you tell if the evidence has captured the conclusion or allowed it to go free?

Let's look at a sample of the strongest kind of argument, something called a valid syllogism.

1. Socrates is a human.

2. All humans are mortal.

3. Therefore, Socrates is a mortal.

The evidence of 1 and 2 completely captures 3. The evidence is a perfect noose for the conclusion. As a matter of fact, if you look closely, you will see that the evidence is merely a longer version of the conclusion. The evidence, as evidence, has already captured the conclusion. If every human is a mortal and if Socrates is a human, then these two statements entirely contain the conclusion that Socrates is a mortal. In a perfectly strong argument such as a valid syllogism, having the evidence means you automatically have the conclusion.

Now look again at the first Nelly argument.

1. The print of a size 11 shoe was found in the victim's blood.

2. Nelly wears a size 11 shoe.

3. Nelly is the killer.

The evidence, as we noted earlier, does not capture the conclusion. In a weak argument, having the evidence is nothing like having the conclusion.

Descartes, probably, makes no argument as perfect as the valid syllogism and, certainly, no argument as weak as the Nelly argument. However, you can judge the strength and the weakness of his arguments by deciding which of the two sample arguments they resemble. The closer Descartes is to the syllogism end of the scale, the stronger his argument; the closer he is to the Nelly end of the scale, the weaker his argument. When he presents evidence that ensnares his conclusion, he is doing what a philosopher ought to do and what he wants to do. When Descartes' evidence doesn't ensnare his conclusion, then you have caught him in an error, which he is trying his hardest to avoid.

Let's conclude by looking at three finer points that will help you dissect Descartes' arguments.

First, whenever Descartes uses "but" at the start of a sentence, he is introducing a counterargument. As you might guess, a counterargument is an argument offered against a previous argument. To dissect counterarguments, follow the procedures described above. Divide the argument into a conclusion piece and one or more evidence pieces. Use "because" and "therefore" to guide you. Then judge the strength of the argument by seeing how strongly the evidence is tied to the conclusion. Use the syllogism/Nelly scale to help.

Second, as you read Descartes, pay close attention to words that point you toward evidence and conclusions. "Since" and "for" are often synonyms for "because" and thus point to evidence. "Hence," "so," "thus," and "consequently" are synonyms for "therefore" and thus point to conclusions.

Third, and most unfortunately for you, Descartes often leaves out evidence or a conclusion. You perform your surgery and find a missing organ. On these occasions, *you must state the unstated.*

For example, here is an argument from Descartes.

"But, I have occasionally caught the senses deceiving me, and it's prudent never completely to trust those who have cheated us even once."

If you try the because/therefore test, you will find the following:

1. "[Because] I have occasionally caught the senses deceiving me,"

2. "[therefore], it's prudent never completely to trust those who have cheated us even once."

But Descartes isn't trying to prove something to us about cheaters. He's trying to prove something to us about the senses. Thus, we have to state the unstated conclusion.

1. "[Because] I have occasionally caught the senses deceiving me," and

2. "[because] it's prudent never completely to trust those who have cheated us even once,"

3. [Therefore, I should not entirely trust my senses.]

You can tell if Descartes has not stated a *conclusion* when the because/therefore test, as it just did above, leads to an irrelevant point. You can suspect that Descartes has not stated *evidence* if the because/therefore test presents an argument that looks too weak. Check to see if the evidence he has presented implies unstated evidence. Then, do the philosophically decent thing. State the unstated.

To sum up, here's how to perform argument surgery.

1. When Descartes appears to be trying to prove something, use the because/therefore test to see if there is a conclusion and evidence.

2. If you find conclusion and evidence, double-check by seeing if the evidence is less obvious than the conclusion.

3. If you don't find conclusion and evidence, see if you need to state the unstated.

4. Judge the strength of the argument by comparing it to the Nelly (weak)/valid syllogism (strong) arguments.

5. Watch carefully for "but," which often introduces a counterargument. Look for "since" and "for" as synonyms for "because"; "hence," "so," "thus," and "consequently" are often synonyms for "therefore."

SUGGESTED READING

Curley, E. M. *Descartes Against the Skeptics*. Cambridge: Harvard University Press, 1978. An argument that "the key feature of Descartes' mature method is its attempt to justify first principles by turning the skeptic's own weapons against him and showing that some propositions are immune to any reasonable doubt."

Frankfurt, Harry G. *Demons, Dreamers and Madmen*. New York: Bobbs-Merrill, 1970. A detailed analysis of the *Meditations* with heavy emphasis on *Meditation I*.

Haldane, Elizabeth S. *Descartes: His Life and Times*. New York: American Scholar Publications, 1966. A classic biography of Descartes.

Hooker, Michael, ed. *Descartes: Critical and Interpretive Essays*. Baltimore: Johns Hopkins University Press, 1978. A collection of essays surveying issues in Descartes' philosophy as a whole.

Lavine, T. Z. *From Socrates to Sartre*. New York: Bantam Books, 1984. The most readable one-volume history of philosophy, with an excellent chapter on Descartes.

Rorty, Amelie Oskenberg, ed. *Essays on Descartes' Meditations*. Berkeley and Los Angeles: University of California Press, 1986. A good sampling of modern critical analysis of the *Meditations*.